The COLETTE SEWING HANDBOOK

INSPIRED STYLES *and* CLASSIC TECHNIQUES *for the* NEW SEAMSTRESS

SARAI MITNICK

KRAUSE PUBLICATIONS
CINCINNATI, OHIO

TABLE OF CONTENTS

THE NEW SEAMSTRESS–6
THE SEWING EXPERIENCE–8
THE FIVE FUNDAMENTALS–9

CHAPTER 1: GETTING STARTED –page 10–
Tools and Supplies–12 | *More Tools and Supplies–14*
Basic Stitches–15 | *Sewing Lessons–18*

CHAPTER 2: A THOUGHTFUL PLAN –page 28–
Inspiration–30 | *Editing for Your Style–32*
Strategy–36 | *A Personalized Croquis–37*

CHAPTER 3: A PRECISE PATTERN –page 38–
Pattern Language–40 | *Prepare Your Fabric–42*
Lay Out Your Pattern–44 | *Transfer the Markings–48*
Cut Your Fabric–50
PROJECT: MERINGUE SKIRT–52

CHAPTER 4: A FANTASTIC FIT –page 60–
What is a Good Fit?–62 | *Ease–64* | *Darts and Fullness–65*
How to Fit–68 | *Step 1: Measure–70* | *Step 2: Trace–72*
Step 3: Make a Muslin–73 | *Step 4: Adjust the Muslin–74*
Step 5: Alter the Pattern–77 | *Types of Alterations–78*
PROJECT: PASTILLE DRESS–90

CHAPTER 5: A BEAUTIFUL FABRIC *-page 102-*
Choosing Fabric—104 | *Fabric Basics—108*
Warp, Weft and Grain—110 | *Common Fabrics—112* | *Interfacing—115*
Thread—116 | *Needles—117*
Prints and Pattern—118 | *Tricky Fabrics—120*
PROJECT: TRUFFLE DRESS—122

CHAPTER 6: A FINE FINISH *-page 134-*
Seam Finishes—136 | *Lining—143*
PROJECT: TAFFY BLOUSE—146

CHAPTER 7: KEEP LEARNING *-page 154-*
Recommended Reading—156
PROJECT: LICORICE DRESS—158

GLOSSARY—170

INDEX—172

SIZE CHART—173

THE NEW SEAMSTRESS

Women come to the idea of making their own clothing for a variety of reasons. Some of us want clothes that fit better, some crave unusual things we can't find in shops, some want to make the luxurious items we can't afford to buy, some are intrigued by the technical aspects of the craft itself. But there's one thing I've found most garment sewers have in common: an interest in clothes. I don't mean an interest in high fashion necessarily, but each budding seamstress has enough of a fascination with clothing to first pick up a needle and thread and say, "I want to make that."

After all, a love of adornment is one of our most basic human tendencies. It exists in all cultures, telling stories about who we are and how we see ourselves. Clothing fills our desire for beauty, for change, for identity, for creativity and play. Not to mention, you interact with it constantly, bringing all those wonderful qualities of beauty and fun into your everyday life. What could be better?

But I've found that there is a dark side to fashion. While it can be an amazing creative outlet, it can also fuel an almost endless desire to consume, to buy more things and to buy them less thoughtfully. With the advent of "fast fashion" in recent years, this is only getting worse, as stores turn over stock and bring in new fashion every few weeks rather than months. Advertisements inundate us with the message that we need newer, trendier items, and more of them. Soon, we're not sure what our own taste is anymore, or how much we really want to own. We have closets of stuff and nothing to wear. Worse, our clothes feel like commodities, with no relationship to who we are.

For me, sewing has been an antidote to this rushing whirlwind of fashion and consumerism. It reclaims fashion as an opportunity for creativity, joy and self-expression. It's taught me about quality, and why I'm drawn to some things and not others. It's given me a more thoughtful approach to my wardrobe, to my own tastes and even my own body. It lets me have fun with clothing, but do it on my own terms.

They say that acquiring more things will never make you happy, but that acquiring experiences can. Being able to make your own wardrobe, to dress exactly the way you choose, and the constant learning that accompanies it is an experience like no other.

THE SEWING EXPERIENCE

I like to sew in the evenings. Since I'm a pattern designer by trade, I'm surrounded by sewing all day long in my studio as I work on new designs, make up samples or write about sewing for my website. Even so, there are few things I find more relaxing then packing up work for the day, making a cup of tea and working on some personal sewing projects before heading home for dinner. It's my favorite way to unwind.

One evening, I had a bit of hand sewing to do. Since I was planning a trip to Argentina, I thought it might be fun to download some Spanish lessons and try them out while I set to work with needle and thread. The first lesson began slowly, covering basic words and greetings that were familiar to me, but also explaining some of the nuances of pronunciation and culture. The pace was relaxed, but it gave me an opportunity to learn some subtleties of the language. In short, they were excellent.

The Spanish instructor mentioned that the lessons were gradual for a reason, so that you should feel relaxed while doing them. He pointed out that a relaxed state is truly the best way to learn a language.

This same wisdom applies to sewing. Learning to sew clothing and learning a new language are both complex skills that take time to develop. They also both involve slowly building up from a foundation of very simple, basic ideas. It is those basic ideas that take you the farthest, because they are the ones you use every day as you build your skills. They are the ones you return to, even when your skill set becomes more advanced.

Just as there are many ways to learn a language, there are also many ways to learn to sew. In this book, I'd like to help you build up and reinforce that foundation of skills. My goal is simple: that you feel good about what you're making and love the experience of sewing.

THE CURIOUS SEAMSTRESS

The Colette Sewing Handbook is intended as a resource for any adventurous, beginning sewer who wants to branch out, as well as intermediate sewers who'd like to brush up their skills with a new, more thoughtful approach.

There's only one trait I think every sewer should possess: curiosity. Learning to sew is an ongoing process; in fact, the learning never really stops. Each project has the potential to teach you something new. Even seamstresses who have been sewing for thirty years or more will tell you that they learn new things all the time. Let your curiosity guide you, and this will be a source of wonder rather than discouragement. A curious person who likes to learn will never get bored with sewing!

Of course, there are other characteristics that are helpful to a sewer. You don't need to be a naturally patient person, although I'm sure it helps. I wouldn't know, I'm highly impulsive and impatient by nature. When I get an idea in my head, I want it done *now*. But sewing has actually taught me patience, how to slow down and do things the right way, and that it's much easier (and more rewarding) to learn to do something right than to fix a mistake over and over. Let your curiosity battle your impatience. Instead of asking "How can I get this done faster?", ask "How can I learn to do this better?"

Attention to detail is another helpful characteristic to have, and one that can be learned. The more you sew, and the more you think about clothing, the more you will notice. Soon the details will become part of your sewing vocabulary.

THE FIVE FUNDAMENTALS

I take a holistic approach to sewing based on what I consider the five ingredients for a remarkable sewing experience: Forming a plan, using a pattern, choosing fabric, customizing the fit and finishing your garment well. While most sewing books focus purely on techniques, these essentials often get overlooked, especially in the beginning of a sewing education. You may learn to sew a dart, but you don't learn why darts are so important to the fit of your garment. In other words, I'd like to tell you a bit about the "why," not just the "how." That way, you'll be better equipped to keep asking questions, to keep learning, and to teach yourself as you go.

There are many books that cover a wide range of sewing techniques, and there are books that focus on a specific technical aspect of sewing. These are both useful types of books to have in your sewing library, and you'll find several of them in the Recommended Reading section (page 156) at the end of this book.

But this book is a little different. We are going to look at the real fundamentals, the actual factors that make a sewing project feel successful and satisfying. Each chapter will cover a different principle, followed by a sewing project that will give you the opportunity to try out your skills. Even if you decide not to make all of the projects in the book, I highly recommend finishing up each chapter with a sewing project that will allow you to try your new skills. Combining these fundamentals with hands-on learning will give you an incredible boost and much more confidence.

A THOUGHTFUL PLAN

In chapter two, we'll cover some basic techniques for designing your sewing projects, and keeping yourself from getting overwhelmed at the fabric store. We'll talk about building from inspiration, considering your own personal style in sewing, and devising a sewing strategy. I'll even show you how to make a personalized croquis based on your own body, which you can use for sketching.

A PRECISE PATTERN

Next, we'll discuss the blueprint of your project, the sewing pattern. I'll explain how to read the markings, prepare your fabric, mark and cut. Then you'll apply those techniques in sewing the Meringue skirt, a simple straight skirt with a flattering shape and pretty scalloped hem.

A FANTASTIC FIT

The ultimate challenge for any sewer is getting the right fit. You don't need to rely on patterns fitting you right out of the box. With a few simple techniques and some patience, you can learn the fundamentals of getting a fit you're happy with. Then you can try it out on a lovely cap-sleeved dress.

A BEAUTIFUL FABRIC

Playing with fabric is one of the creative highlights of sewing. Just like a painter must learn about the differences between acrylics, oils and watercolor, you'll learn about the medium of textiles. We'll cover the various dimensions and qualities of fabric, so you'll be able to imagine even more possibilities. At the end of this chapter, you'll try a dress with a special asymmetric drape that will get you thinking about applying these qualities to a real project.

A FINE FINISH

Finishing puts that last touch on a well-made garment. You'll learn about a variety of seam finishes for a more professional result, how to pair finishes with fabric, and all about linings. You'll be able to sew a bias-cut blouse with bound edges.

BRINGING IT ALL TOGETHER

Finally, we'll wrap up with a slightly more complex project: a lined dress that will help you combine many of the book's lessons and techniques, and really solidifies your understanding of the five fundamentals.

Chapter One

GETTING STARTED

There's a term in French for the preparations a chef makes before she begins cooking: "mise en place." Literally, it means "putting in place," and it refers to the way professionals assemble everything that's needed before beginning to cook. The chef will review the recipe, assemble the necessary tools, prepare any ingredients, and make sure anything needed is close at hand.

This first chapter is dedicated to the concept of *mise en place*. It can reduce stress and mistakes in the sewing room, just as it does in the kitchen. First, you want to make sure your sewing area is set up with the proper tools and equipment. We'll cover the basic tools and supplies you should have, as well as a few nice-to-haves you may want to pick up.

Once you have your tools and supplies, your next step is making sure any techniques you may need are well understood before you start a project. Even if a technique is new to you, it's a good idea to review it and make sure it clicks before you try applying it for the first time. To that end, this chapter has several lessons on basic techniques you'll use frequently in sewing. You can review them now and refer back to them as you start a new project. In fact, each project in this book has a "skills checklist" that will refer back to the pages with relevant lessons throughout the book.

Let the concept of *mise en place* guide you, and sewing will suddenly become much more relaxing. With that in mind, let's get set up.

TOOLS AND SUPPLIES

I believe in making things easy on yourself and eliminating frustration before it starts whenever you can. The easiest way to do that is to start your work with the right tools. This will not only give you better results, it will also make sewing much more pleasurable. Collect tools that help boost your confidence.

Many of the problems you might face in sewing are really just a matter of not having the right tool for the job. Many times, you'll discover a new little sewing tool that makes short work of a technique you've struggled with for months or years. These gadgets can be a lot of fun to collect, but first there are a few basics that will take you pretty far on their own. Start with these and then explore.

THREAD, PINS AND NEEDLES

Needles and thread are, of course, the most basic tools for sewing. Having a small arsenal means you'll be stocked up for any project you dream up.

THREAD

Most fabrics will use all-purpose polyester thread, but sometimes cotton is a good choice. Silk is used most often for hand sewing and basting. Topstitching thread is a decorative thread. For more details, see chapter five.

PINS

I like pearl-head pins as they're easy to spot. If you plan to sew with light silks, pick up some silk pins, which are finer and won't leave large holes.

HAND SEWING NEEDLES

Keep several sizes on hand, using finer needles for lighter fabrics and thicker needles for heavy fabrics.

MACHINE NEEDLES

Again, you will need several varieties, so that you can match the needle to the fabric. See chapter five for a needle chart to match thread and fabric.

THIMBLE

Thimbles protect your fingertip, allowing you to more easily push a hand sewing needle through your fabric.

PIN CUSHION

Some people prefer magnetic pin cushions, or pin cushions you wear around your wrist. I like the old-fashioned tomato cushion. The little strawberry shape that dangles off of it is filled with emery sand that you can use to sharpen your pins just by pushing them in and out.

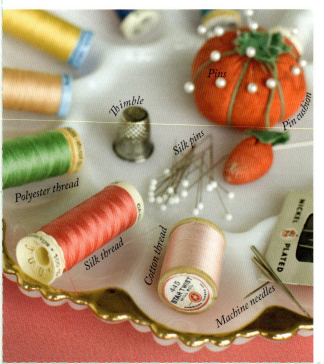

CUTTING, MEASURING AND MARKING TOOLS

You'll also need a few tools for cutting out your pattern and fabric, taking measurements and making adjustments, and transferring pattern markings.

DRESSMAKER'S SHEARS
Use these specialty shears to cut fabric, and fabric only. Get them sharpened regularly and you'll be rewarded with a comfortable tool that glides through fabric.

PAPER SCISSORS
Just your standard scissors, which you can use to cut your pattern.

ROTARY CUTTER (OPTIONAL)
A rotary cutter can make cutting go twice as fast, and it is quite precise. It does require a cutting mat, which is the expensive part. Buy the biggest mat you can afford and you will never look back.

THREAD NIPPERS (OPTIONAL)
Keep nippers on hand to snip off thread as you sew. I sometimes wear mine on a ribbon around my neck when I'm sewing.

SEAM RIPPER
When mistakes happen (and they will), your seam ripper will be there to help you start again.

CLEAR RULER
Clear bendable 18" (45.7cm) rulers make measuring and marking very easy.

MEASURING TAPE
You'll use a flexible measuring tape for measuring so many things while you sew, but it's especially useful for body measurements.

FRENCH CURVE
This is basically a curved ruler. You will use it to draw curves if you make any pattern alterations.

MARKING PENS AND CHALK
Use these for marking your fabric before sewing. You should have an assortment on hand, since different fabrics work best with different marking tools. I like chalk pens the best.

TRACING WHEEL (OPTIONAL)
You can use a tracing wheel along with dressmaker's paper, which is sort of like carbon paper, to transfer markings to your fabric.

MORE TOOLS AND SUPPLIES

PRESSING TOOLS

Pressing is the most overlooked aspect of sewing, but makes a huge difference to your end result. A few tools will help make those seams and hems crisp and lovely.

STEAM IRON

Look for an iron with good, adjustable steam and temperature. This will allow you to fine-tune the amount of moisture and heat you need for different fabrics.

SEAM ROLL

A seam roll is a large, firm tube. You lay the seam along the fabric roll and press. This way, the seam allowance is held away from the fabric while you're pressing, and won't cause impressions. It can also be inserted into sleeves when pressing.

TAILOR'S HAM

This rounded wedge is placed under curved areas when you press, helping you to shape them.

PRESS CLOTH

A press cloth protects your fabric from the surface of the iron. Lay it over your fabric before you press to avoid scorching or shine marks. You can cut one yourself from an old sheet.

POINT TURNER

A point turner can help get those sharp points you want on corners, such as the point of a collar. After you've stitched a point and want to turn it right side out, place the point turner inside the tip. Turn your piece right side out around the point turner, holding it in place with your fingers as you turn. You can also use the point turner to nudge out the edges of points and seams before you press them. Because bamboo is a fairly soft wood, there's less chance of poking holes in your seams.

BASIC STITCHES

MACHINE STITCHES

While different machines come with different stitches, there are really only a few that are essential to most modern sewing. The straight stitch is what you will use most of the time, while the zigzag will often come in handy. Other stitches are nice to have, but not quite as essential.

STRAIGHT

This is the most basic stitch, and the one you're likely to use the most.

ZIGZAG

The zigzag stitch moves the needle left and right as you sew. This stitch has more elasticity, so you can use it to sew seams on knits. It's also used for sewing on appliqué or lace, or even for decorative effect.

OVERLOCK

The overlock stitch simulates the stitch of the serger machine, to finish raw edges.

BLIND STITCH

This stitch is used for creating a blind hem, a type of hem that can barely be seen on the right side.

DECORATIVE STITCHES

Many machines come with decorative stitches that you can use to embellish your sewing.

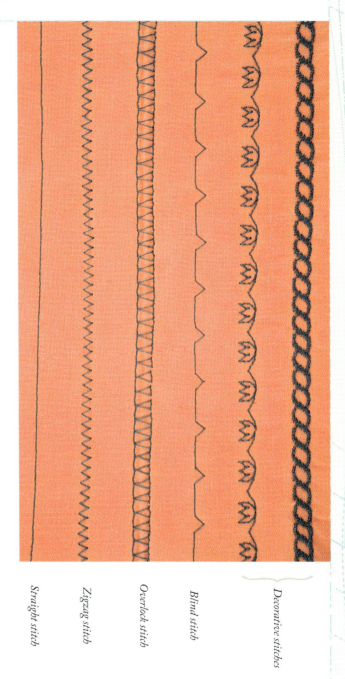

Straight stitch | *Zigzag stitch* | *Overlock stitch* | *Blind stitch* | *Decorative stitches*

HAND STITCHES

While we aren't used to seeing hand stitches in most of our store-bought clothing, they are used frequently in couture sewing because they give the sewer so much control and can produce incredible results. Since home sewers don't have all the fancy specialized equipment that allows ready-to-wear manufacturers to skip the hand sewing, why not embrace the couture methods? Use silk thread for hand basting or sewing your hems by hand for an invisible finish.

RUNNING STITCH

This is the most basic hand stitch. A running stitch with long stitches is used for hand basting (sometimes referred to as a "basting stitch").

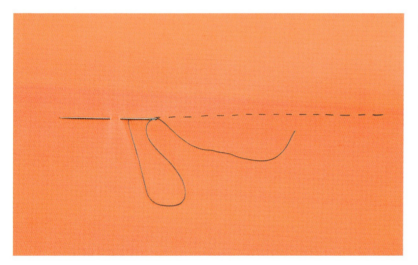

Anchor the thread, and work the needle in and out evenly before pulling the thread through.

BACKSTITCH

The backstitch is a very strong stitch, used for permanently joining seams.

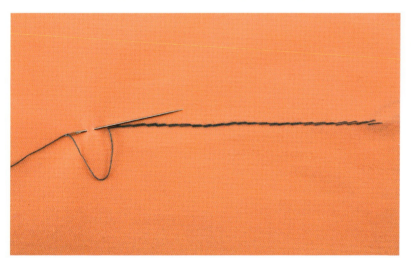

Anchor the thread. Insert the needle 1/16" (2mm) to the right of the working thread and pull it out 1/16" (2mm) in front of the working thread. Continue in this way, always bringing the needle back over the space you created.

CATCHSTITCH

The catchstitch is often used on hems. It is inconspicuous and will hold two layers flat against one another, such as when you're sewing a hem.

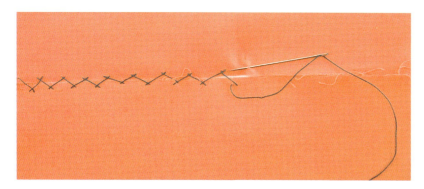

Anchor the thread. Insert the needle from right to left in one layer, creating a small horizontal stitch. Move down and the right in the second layer, and take another stitch from right to left. Continue, moving from left to right, but with the tip of the needle always pointing to the left.

WHIPSTITCH

The whipstitch is often used to create a very narrow seam. You might use it to attach lace, for example.

Insert the needle from back to front, a little below the edge. Pass the needle over the edge and insert again from back to front, to the left of the previous stitch.

SLIPSTITCH

The slipstitch is used to hold a fold against a piece of fabric. It is another inconspicuous stitch that is used in hemming.

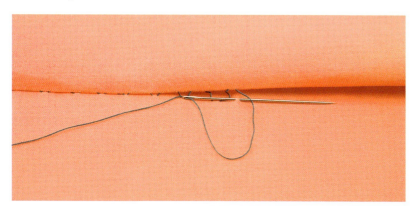

Pass the needle through the fold, bringing it out again through the edge of the fold. Take a tiny stitch in the flat fabric, catching just a few threads of fabric. Insert again into the fold and pass along within the fold to start the next stitch.

SEWING LESSONS

Let's get started with some basic lessons in technique! Take a look through these methods for a starter course on common sewing tasks. Of course, we aren't covering every possible sewing technique here, but you'll find that these come up very frequently in garment sewing. These breakdowns are here for you to reference whenever you need a little refresher.

PRESSING A SEAM OPEN

Press each and every seam after you sew it. This is the only way to get flat, inconspicuous seams. Most seams are pressed open, but if your pattern calls for a seam to be pressed to the side, follow these same steps, but move the seam allowance to one side before pressing on the wrong side.

1. Press the seam as it was sewn. This helps set the stitches.

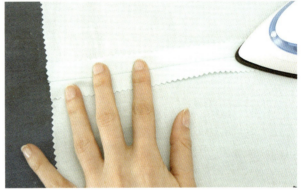

2. Open up your fabric and lay it wrong-side up. Press along the seam, flattening the seam allowance. If your fabric is delicate, you may wish to lay the seam on a seam roll, to avoid marks from the seam allowance.

3. Turn so that the right side is up. Press the seam again from the right side.

PRESSING VERSUS IRONING

Be aware that pressing is different from ironing. Ironing involves moving the iron back and forth over your fabric. When pressing, you hold the iron still and apply pressure.

HOW TO GATHER

Gathers give a garment soft fullness around a seam, or they can be used to create basic ruffles. I use three rows of basting to create very even gathers, rather than the usual two rows. Take care to avoid uneven gathers or any pleats in the fabric when stitching.

1. Using the longest stitch length on your machine and with right side up, sew three rows of basting stitches ⅛" (30cm) apart. I like to sew one just on the inside of the seamline, one on the seamline, and the other on the outside of the seamline. Leave long thread tails.

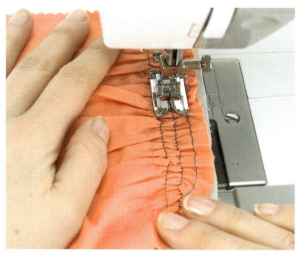

2. On the wrong side, pull the bobbin thread tails to gather the fabric. Slide the fabric along the thread to distribute the gathers evenly.

3. Stitch your seam, stitching over the gathers. Stitch with the gathered side up, so you can see what you're doing, and adjust the fabric if necessary. Remove the basting thread and press.

HOW TO SEW A DART

Darts are the foundation of garment design, and they are prevalent in many types of clothing. Darts should be smooth, so using a curved surface, like a tailor's ham, when pressing will help you avoid any odd bubbles or points at the tip.

1. Fold the dart through the center, with right sides together, matching up the lines that form the legs of the dart. Pin into place.

2. Begin at the wide end of the dart, backstitching a couple stitches to anchor the thread. Sew through the line to the tip, right off the edge.

3. It's important to secure the thread at the tip of your dart, or it will pull apart during normal washing and wearing. Tying off the end is an easy way to do this, and doesn't cause the slight bumps that backstitching might. To tie off thread, simply leave long thread tails at the tip of your dart while sewing. After you've stitched the dart, tie the two threads at the tip together in a knot and clip the thread tails.

4. Press the dart in the direction the pattern indicates. It's helpful to lay your dart over a tailor's ham to help get the tip nice and flat.

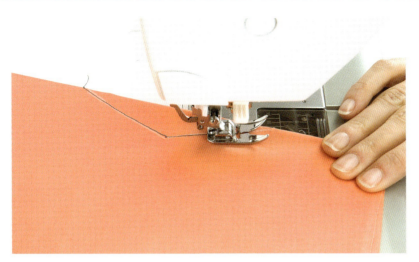

Double-Pointed Darts

For a double-pointed dart, sew as if you're sewing two darts, starting in the middle and working out to a tip, then returning to the middle and sewing to the other tip. You may need to clip the dart in the center to help it lay flat when you press it, or even clip it in a few spots depending on the curve. Double pointed darts are often found in dresses, jackets or tops without a waistline seam. You'll use double-pointed darts in the Licorice Dress (page 158).

TUCKS

Tucks are similar to darts, except that instead of a wedge shape that tapers to a point, a tuck is sewn in a straight line. The fabric has a soft fold at the end, similar to the look of a pleated skirt. To sew a tuck, bring the stitching lines together with right sides together and pin, just like you did with the dart. Stitch from the edge toward the other end. When you reach the end of the stitching line, pivot 90 degrees and sew across the tuck, right off the edge. Press tucks just up to the stitching line for a soft fold.

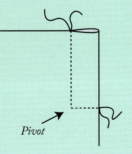

Pivot

HOW TO INSTALL A FACING

When I was brand new to sewing, I thought curved areas like necklines and armholes could be finished in the same way as a skirt hem: just turn it under and stitch. Of course, anyone who's tried this knows that it just doesn't work. The result puckers and twists horribly, if you can sew it at all. Enter the facing, a little piece that mirrors the curve exactly. Grading the seams prevents adding too much bulk, while understitching keeps the facing from rolling forward. You simply sew it along the curved area, then turn it to the inside!

1. With right sides together, pin the facing to the opening, aligning any notches or seams. Stitch into place. To grade the seam allowance, trim the seam allowance of the facing only, so it is half the width of the other seam allowance. Making the seam allowances two different widths will make the seam less bulky. Clip the seam allowance along any inward curves (such as on a neckline), or notch if there are outward curves.

2. Now you will understitch. Press the seam allowance toward the facing. Stitch the seam allowance to the facing, close to the seamline.

3. Turn the facing to the inside when you are done, and press.

CLIPPING AND NOTCHING

When a seam is curved, turning it the inside can cause pulling or wrinkling. To make curved seams lay flat, use the tips of your shears to notch or clip the seam allowance, taking care not to cut into the stitching.

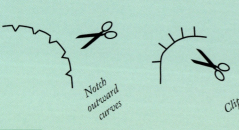

Notch outward curves

Clip inward curves

HOW TO INSTALL AN INVISIBLE ZIPPER

Invisible zippers are my favorite closures for most garments. If you have an invisible zipper foot, they're easy to install and look clean and professional.

1. Prepping your zipper by pressing the coils flat lets you stitch a little closer to the teeth. You'll notice that the teeth of the zipper pull to the back. Unzip your zipper and, using a low heat setting and the tip of your iron, press the zipper near the teeth so that it is flat.

2. Begin with a seam that has not been sewn yet (you should have two separate pieces). On each piece, mark the seamline where the zipper will be installed. The easiest way to do this is with a row of machine basting. With the right side of the zipper against the fabric's right side, place the zipper along the seam as shown, aligning the teeth of the zipper with the seamline. Pin or baste in place.

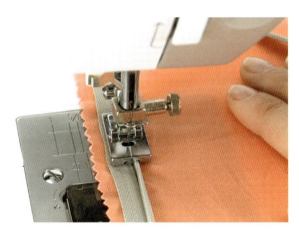

3. Stitch into place using your invisible zipper foot, stitching close to the teeth. Stop when you reach the zipper pull at the bottom. Notice that the teeth of the zipper fit neatly in the groove of the invisible zipper foot.

4. Aligning the other side of the zipper with the seamline of the other side, pin and stitch into place in the same way, making sure the zipper will close before you stitch and that it's not twisted. Finish by stitching the rest of the seam closed below the zipper.

HOW TO INSTALL A CENTERED ZIPPER

Centered zippers are the most basic type of zipper closure, and work well for many garments. Use this method to sew in a zipper with less fuss and no ugly gaping.

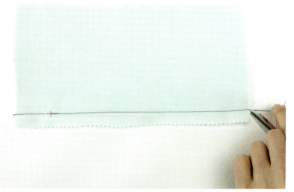

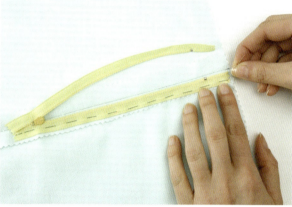

1. Sew the seam up to the point where the zipper will end. Using a long stitch length, machine-baste the opening where the zipper will be installed, so it is temporarily closed. Press the seam open.

2. Open up the zipper and place it face-down on the opening you've basted closed on the wrong side. On the fist side, move the zipper teeth very slightly from the basted edge and hand-baste into place. Moving the teeth just slightly from the center will help hide the teeth.

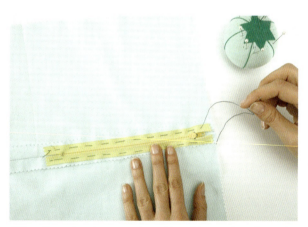

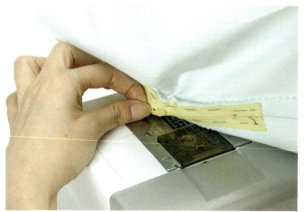

3. Close the zipper again and hand-baste the other side, rolling the zipper slightly so that the teeth are offset on this side as well.

4. Open the zipper again. On the right side of the garment, use a zipper foot to stitch down one side of the zipper, stopping about two-thirds of the way, with your needle in the down position. Lift the presser foot and close the zipper (shown). This way, you do not have to stitch around the pull tab. Continue to the end on this side.

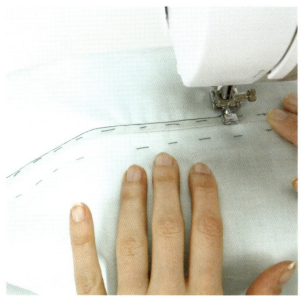

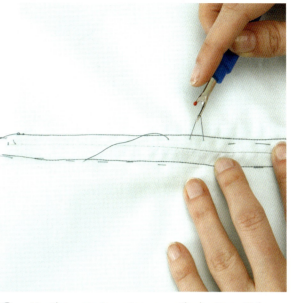

5. Pivot and sew a small line of stitches across the bottom of the zipper. Return to the top and sew the other side down in the same manner.

6. Use the seam ripper to remove the basting stitches along the sides of the zipper.

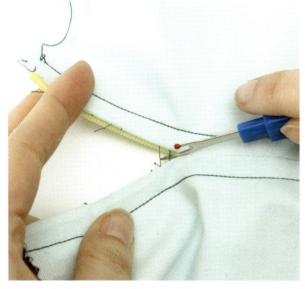

7. Unzip the zipper, and then use the seam ripper to remove the machine-basted stitches down the center of the seam.

ZIPPER LENGTH

You can easily shorten any zipper by stitching a few stitches back and forth over the teeth. Use a zigzag stitch, the biggest width, and a short or 0 stitch length to create a bartack that acts as a new zipper stop. So if you can't find the right length, go a little longer than you need.

HOW TO SET A SLEEVE

Set-in sleeves are very common in women's clothing. It seems tricky at first because you begin with two curved seams that don't match up exactly. The sleeve seam will usually be a little longer than the armhole seam, so you will need to ease the sleeve to fit. Easing is similar to gathering, but less fabric is drawn up by the stitches before you sew. The easing gives a soft roundness to the top of the sleeve.

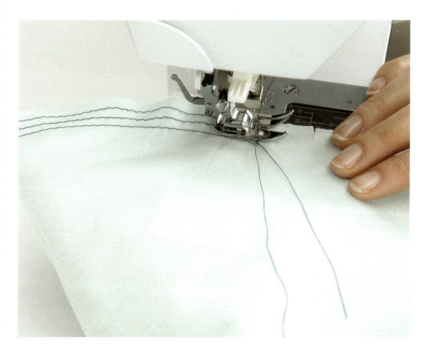

1. On your sleeve, using the longest stitch length on your machine and with right side up, sew three rows of basting stitches ⅛" (30mm) apart. The middle row of basting should be right on the seamline. These will be used for easing the sleeve cap.

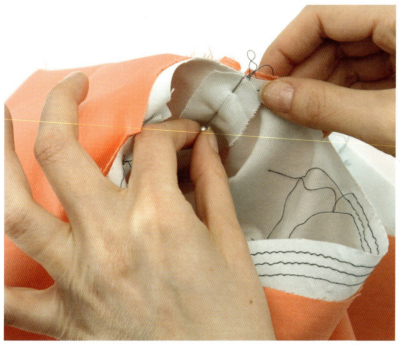

2. With right sides together, pin the sleeve into the armhole. To do this, you will turn your garment wrong side out, then insert the sleeve into the armhole. Align any notches and seams, and pin from the sleeve side up to the points where the basting starts.

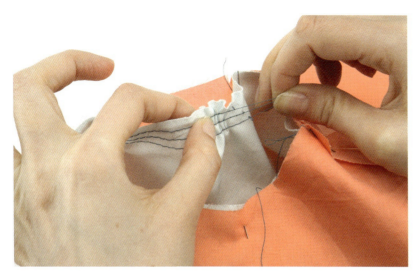

3. Pull the thread tails on the basting to draw up the fabric, making the sleeve the same length as the armhole. Adjust the easing so that it is even, and pin in place using plenty of pins. Again, pin from the sleeve side.

4. Stitch the sleeve into the armhole, stitching from the sleeve side. This way you'll be able to see the easing and make sure no fabric gets tucked or folded as it's stitched.

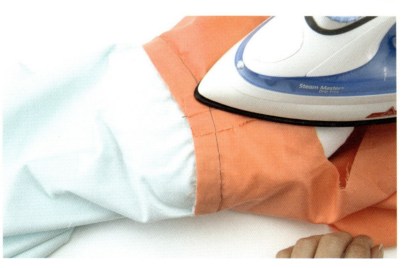

5. Remove basting. Clip the seam allowance along the underarm curve (see page 22). Press the seam toward the sleeve, using a tailor's ham inserted in the sleeve to press the curves. You should have a slight fullness at the top of the sleeve.

Chapter Two

A THOUGHTFUL PLAN

We have no shortage of choice when it comes to picking what we want to wear. With constantly rotating trends, new looks, and "must-haves" every season, the simple act of dressing yourself can often feel overwhelming. We're constantly urged to try new styles, and it's true that they can be exciting and fun. But if you're anything like me, deep down, all you really want is a closet filled with your favorite things. These are the clothes that make you happy to put on, that make you feel like yourself. Instead, many of us feel that we have a closet stuffed with clothes and nothing we want to wear.

You would think that being able to sew your own clothing would solve this particular issue. After all, you can pretty much make exactly what you want, right? Unfortunately, sewing clothing seems to magnify this problem. Once you start sewing, you can make almost any style in nearly any color or any fabric. Shell buttons or wood? A solid fabric or a print? Silk or cotton? If I get overwhelmed at the clothing store, you should see me buying fabric. It's very easy to make mistakes when you are surrounded by lush prints, radiant colors and every texture imaginable.

The real solution is to take the time to do a little thoughtful editing, to think about your own life and style and focus on making the things you will truly love. My approach is to focus on quality over quantity. With all of the possibilities out there, it's tempting to rush from one sewing project to another, trying somehow to capture all of your ideas. But this frantic approach to sewing just mimics the confusion of always buying new clothes. Instead, editing your ideas, taking your time with each one, and thinking carefully about what you want to make is more likely to yield a garment you will cherish.

INSPIRATION

Most of us who take up sewing are highly visual, tactile people. We love to feel the texture of fabrics, to try out unexpected combinations of color, and to imagine details and trims. As much as I enjoy the construction process, turning inspiration into a concrete plan is the really exciting part for me.

In the past, you may have felt like planning a sewing project was just a matter of combining a pattern you like with a pretty fabric. But I invite you to think about it more as a design process. It might start with a pattern or a fabric, or it might be inspired by a piece of art or a photograph. Like any exercise in design, it's really a matter of looking at lots of possibilities and then making editing decisions.

My planning method has three steps: inspiration, editing and strategy.

The first step is gathering inspiration. This means capturing anything that inspires you or sparks an idea and keeping it for later. Keeping track of the things that inspire you will help you to understand your taste over time, and ensure that none of your great ideas get lost.

FINDING INSPIRATION

What inspires you? The fashion-conscious among us might look to the runways for inspiration, and they can be a terrific source of ideas, but there's no reason to limit yourself to the current trends. Look to the world at large and see what intrigues you personally. You can probably list a host of influences on your personal taste and style, and these are often a great place to start. Some ideas where inspiration often lurks:

YOUR CLOSET
Take a look at the clothing you already own and love. Think about what makes it really special or right for you.

VINTAGE GARMENTS
Much of the designer clothing we see today incorporates elements from the past. Vintage clothing often has details that are rarely seen in mass-produced modern clothing.

MUSEUMS AND FINE ART
From Greek sculpture to abstract paintings, fine art has always influenced fashion. I love to turn again and again to my favorite artists when I'm dreaming up ideas or thinking about color.

FILM
It could be the movie costumes of Edith Head, or the latest Sofia Coppola film.

FABRIC AND TRIM
I love to collect swatches of fabric and see what ideas they spark in time. Sometimes raw materials are the only inspiration you need to get going.

TRAVEL
There's nothing quite like immersing yourself in the style and landscape of another place. Even if you can't travel much, you can find street style blogs from all over the world showcasing looks in other cities.

KEEPING INSPIRATION

Inspiration can be found anywhere, but there's something about the process of keeping track of it that changes the way you see things. You begin to notice the possibilities more and to think about the way things affect you. It's a way to reflect, but also a way to formulate and refine your ideas.

Sketchbooks and notebooks are a necessity in my life, and I carry around a small one in my bag at all times. Whenever an idea strikes, I get it down on paper for future reference. My little black notebook contains everything from a hasty sketch of a chic woman I saw on the Paris Metro to a little diagram of an interesting sleeve placket I came across in a tailor's shop in San Francisco. Sometimes I paste in photos, images, or swatches. When I return to flip through my notebooks, I'm greeted with a wealth of ideas and inspiring memories.

When it comes time to formulate a plan, I love to create mood boards. Mood boards can help focus your ideas, letting you build your inspiration around a specific look or theme. They are incredibly helpful if you have an ambitious sewing goal, such as planning a new winter wardrobe, or several pieces you want to sew for an upcoming vacation. Your board might include images that represent the look you want, sketches, accessories, color palettes, fabric swatches or trims.

Gathering Inspiration
Sketchbooks, notebooks and scrapbooks help you catalog and remember your ideas.

Inspiration to Grow On
Studying how clothing is constructed is a good way to become inspired. Vintage dresses in particular can inspire you to try new techniques. If you study them closely, their fine details and interesting construction can trigger your curiosity and motivate you to learn something new.

Processing Inspiration
Mood boards can help you process your inspiration into a solid idea.

EDITING FOR YOUR STYLE

Once you have plenty of inspiration, the second step is to make some editing decisions based on what you will actually wear, and what fits your life. For me, this is usually a mental process of asking myself a few questions as I go through my inspiration sources. You might also choose to jot down notes or even start sketching more concrete ideas.

It's important to think critically about your own style and tastes before you start sewing. Sewing gives you an opportunity to express who you are in your daily life like almost nothing else can. Rather than assembling a wardrobe from the clothing you find, you can design your own style based only on the things you love, that say something about who you are. I find this to be one of the greatest gifts sewing has to offer: the chance to bring artistry into your everyday life and to express yourself creatively with the things you make. Not only can you make something beautiful, but you can make something beautiful that says something about who you are, and you can use it in your real life. In that sense, sewing is truly a practical art.

DRESSING FOR YOURSELF

Some styles of clothing just feel right when you put them on. They're comfortable, they fit your personality, and they match your taste in just the right way. They work with who you are and reflect your favorite qualities out into the world. At the same time, there are other styles that you might like, but never feel quite right when you put them on. Distinguishing between the things that feel like you and the things that don't is the only real secret to developing a strong sense of style, one that means something to you.

Consider the people you believe to have the best personal style, whether they're famous style icons or people from your own life. You've probably noticed that they have pretty specific tastes. They know what they like, and they're true to themselves as individuals. They cherry-pick the colors, textures and shapes that speak to them and work with who they are.

I believe in a personal approach to style. To me, that means wearing the things that make you happy. This takes a bit of reflection and a dash of restraint. It means recognizing the things you like on others, but that may not work for you. It means probing yourself a little, asking yourself why certain kinds of clothes make you feel good.

Try going into your closet and picking out five things that you love to wear. It might include a ring given to you by your grandmother, your coziest sweater, your simplest black dress or bright turquoise shoes. Why do you feel so strongly about these things? What is it that makes them special to you? What feelings do they provoke? By understanding what you value in the things you love, you can begin to imagine a whole wardrobe of personal clothing, built around the qualities that are important to you.

It may help to describe the qualities that appeal to you the most. Make a list of words that describe the aesthetics of your favorite things. You might also include the fabrics you love, the colors that work for you or the kinds of shapes you like to wear. You don't need to put yourself in a box, but can still be helpful to recognize that you are drawn to things that are "dark, mysterious, romantic, feminine" or "minimalist, practical, androgynous, sleek." You might even take a photo of the things you have that best express your own style. Remembering that you love neutrals may make it easier to put down that enticing tropical print at the fabric store.

Organic, natural, earthy

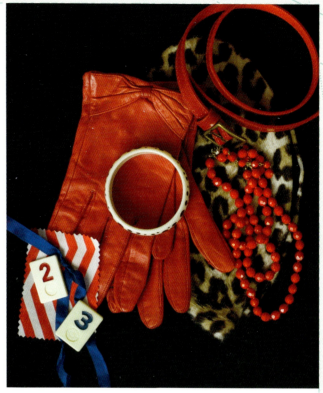

Bright, bold, graphic

Sparkling, glamorous, feminine

Classic, simple, understated

DRESSING FOR YOUR LIFE

Even when we understand the sort of things we are drawn to, many of us face a separate wardrobe challenge: acquiring clothing that fits our lives. I will be the first to admit that in spite of the fact that I ride a bicycle to work much of the time, I own far more party dresses than pairs of jeans.

Of course, it's nice to sew the things we love, but it's even nicer if we can sew things we love and will get to wear. Again, take a look at your closet. You probably have a sense of where the holes are and the sorts of clothes you need more of. Often, it's the practical and mundane clothing that's most neglected, but these are sometimes the things we wear the most. Stretch your imagination and try to think of creative ways to fill these gaps with things that still excite you. I may not be a jeans and T-shirt kind of woman, but I find some crisp dark denim and a pretty blouse works for me. Your lifestyle and budget are design constraints, and most designers will tell you that constraints boost creative thinking.

PLANNING QUESTIONS

When deciding on a particular sewing project, try asking yourself these questions:

- *Will I feel good in it?*
- *Will it be comfortable?*
- *What will I wear with it?*
- *How often will I wear it?*

DRESSING FOR YOUR SHAPE

There are many female body types. Yes, sometimes it's helpful to have the shorthand of saying that you are "pear-shaped" or "apple-shaped." But when you get down to it, most of our bodies have numerous quirks beyond what a simple fruit metaphor can represent. Having large hips doesn't mean you don't also have a short torso. You might have a small bust, but also broad shoulders. Our bodies are highly individual, and our feelings about them and how we wish to dress them are, too.

Dressing for your shape can be very subjective. One woman with a large bust may prefer to balance it with a full skirt. Another woman with the same proportions may feel overwhelmed in full skirts and prefer dresses that skim her figure. The truth is, it's largely a matter of taste and how you relate to your body. There are no hard rules, because if you feel good wearing it, there's absolutely no reason not to.

Think about the kinds of shapes that you prefer wearing. Do you like your clothes to be sharp and tailored or soft and drapey? Do you like long skirts or short? Sleek shapes or fullness? Do you feel better when your clothes are very fitted or a bit loose?

There are good reasons that you feel comfortable in certain shapes, and they are probably related to how you think about your body. Do you like tailored jackets because they show off your waist? Do shorter skirts show off your legs? If you feel beautiful in it, there is no reason to listen to general fashion prescriptions. Rules of thumb can sometimes be helpful, but you no doubt have a much better idea of what works for you than any expert. After all, you're the one living in your body.

By the same token, you should think about shapes that make you feel uncomfortable. You don't need to dwell on what you see as your "flaws," but just think about what you truly feel happy wearing. You may love the look of full skirts, but if you feel frumpy in them, there's no reason to waste time sewing them.

tailored *flowing* *fitted* *loose* *short* *long*

Which shapes do you tend to gravitate toward? Which do you feel emphasize the things you like about your body? Which make you most comfortable?

A Fitted, Tailored Sheath

This vintage dress is fitted to the body with darts and seams, making it a more fitted and tailored style. The linen fabric lends itself to the structured look of this very flattering, ladylike dress.

A Flowing, Loose Dress

While this vintage dress is shown on the same body, it has a very different look. It is fitted around the body only with softy gathers at the waist and neck, and the sheer silk fabric flows and moves gracefully. Which would you rather wear?

STRATEGY

Once you've thought a bit about the things you're drawn to, you probably have plenty of ideas about the things you want to make! Now it's time to formulate a concrete plan of attack that will guide your sewing projects and keep you on track.

Not everyone is a planner, and I do think there should be plenty of room for experimentation and the occasional impulse project. But having an overall plan is a great way to ensure that you spend your time and money on things you both love and want to use. After all, sewing is not cheap. Even if you score a great deal on patterns and fabrics, the amount of time it takes to construct a garment makes it expensive in terms of time. So do it thoughtfully and make it a labor of love.

This step is where you go from a general concept to making definite decisions about you pattern, fabric, trims, details you want to add and construction techniques you'd like to try. The form your plan takes is up to you. Some people enjoy planning things on a large scale, while others prefer to take their projects one at a time. This is the method I use to plan my projects, but feel free to pick and choose the methods that will work best for you.

Adding to Your Fashion Sketch
If you know what sewing pattern you will use, you can use the technical drawing on the pattern envelope to draw your sketch. Add notes about fabric, color and other details you plan to use.

DEVELOP YOUR PLAN

DESIGN A SEASONAL WARDROBE. In early fall and early spring, I sift through my inspiration books, folders and images. I'll also look at the fabric and patterns I own, and perhaps take a trip to the fabric store just to gather ideas. I then edit them based on the constraints of my life and sketch a mini-wardrobe of what I'd like to wear that season. It might contain 10 to 15 pieces, some things I already own, some things I plan to buy, and many things I'd like to sew.

MAKE A PROJECT LIST. From my mini-wardrobe, I list the projects I plan to sew in order to create it. I'll add notes on fabric types, patterns and notions.

DRAW A FASHION SKETCH. I use a croquis template to sketch my next project, drawing the lines over the template and adding more specific notes and fabric swatches to fully flesh it out. On the next page, I'll show you how to create your own personalized croquis template.

KEEP A "SOMEDAY" FOLDER. When I have an idea for a "someday" project, I try to capture it. This might be a sketch, or an inspirational photo with notes. This is a little different from an inspiration notebook for me. It's more of a queue of future projects. That way, if I have a great idea but don't have time for it currently, I can be confident that it's been captured, and that I'll return to it the next time I'm planning.

A PERSONALIZED CROQUIS

Designers often begin the design process with a "croquis." This is the term the fashion and sewing industry uses; it comes from the word "sketch" in French. And that is exactly what it is: a sketch of clothing on a figure. You can make use of this technique at home by creating a personal croquis template that's modeled after your own body. With this drawing template at hand, you can easily sketch clothing on your own figure, examining the lines and visualizing the final garment more easily. When you've finalized your sketch, you can add details, such as fabric swatches and notes on trims, transforming your croquis into a concrete sewing plan.

HOW TO MAKE A CROQUIS

We're not all artists, but don't let that stop you. To get an accurate sketch of your body, you can use a camera and simply trace your figure.

1. Begin by putting on clothing that reveals the shape of your body. You might choose dance attire, such as leotards and leggings, or simply wear your normal undergarments.

2. Stand against a plain background and have a friend photograph you, or use the self-timer on your camera. Take a photo straight on, standing in a normal posture.

3. Enlarge the photo to the size you prefer and print it out.

4. Using a fine-point pen or pencil, trace the outlines of your body onto another sheet of paper.

5. Make copies of your template, or scan it into a computer and print more as you need them. You might even put copies into a binder to use as a fashion sketchbook.

6. Sketch designs right onto your figure or, if you prefer, trace the lines to create a new fashion sketch.

37

Chapter Three

A PRECISE PATTERN

*Y*ou have your idea in mind, and your sewing pattern is the blueprint to carry it out. But if that were the whole story, making clothing would be a simple task, just a matter of following directions to the letter. In reality, your task is not just cutting and sewing, but translating between the beautiful image in your head and the actual structure you have laid out for you. Doing that requires a sort of sewing literacy, an ability to read a pattern just as you read written instructions.

The sewing pattern forms the bones of your project, a scaffolding on which you can hang so many of your own ideas. The pattern helps you achieve the structure, which you can personalize for your own tastes and body. We'll discuss customizing a pattern for a perfect fit in chapter four, but first let's explore the pattern itself.

A sewing pattern is basically a template of your garment. The structure of a garment is a pretty difficult thing to develop yourself, even for experienced sewists, so having a starting point is invaluable for home sewing. With a sewing pattern, the designer provides you with what is essentially a paper version of your project in a range of standard sizes, with special marks to show you how to lay out the pattern, how to manipulate it and where to sew. Your job is to use that template to cut and mark your own version before sewing it together. There are many ways to do this, depending on your fabric, your project and your own preferences. Even if you're experienced with sewing patterns, I invite you to take a look at some of the tools and techniques in this chapter and see if there are some you might like to try or revisit.

PATTERN LANGUAGE

Sewing patterns are marked with a sort of visual shorthand made up of a few basic construction symbols. We tend to think that the written instruction sheet or book that comes with a pattern is the source of all directions. But, in fact, the written instructions and the construction symbols on the pattern work together to form a complete set of instructions. That way, the written instructions can refer to specific points or areas of the pattern, and you'll always know exactly where it's referring to.

ARROWS
Grainlines are marked by double-pointed arrows. The arrows on your pattern should always be placed parallel to the long edges of the fabric, in other words the fold or selvages. An arrow bracket that points to the edge of a pattern piece indicates that it should be placed on the fold of the fabric.

NOTCHES
Notches show how seams go together. You will find notches along the cutting lines on your pattern. These help you figure out how the pieces go together. The notches of adjoining pieces should match exactly when they are sewn together. So looking out for them should help stop you from sewing a piece in upside down or in the wrong place.

DARTS
Darts are marked by triangular lines. The lines show where you will stitch the dart together, and are known as the "legs" of the dart. Sometimes the lines are dashed, or there may be circles along the line for you to match up. Single-sided darts usually fall on a seam line, whereas double-sided might be placed anywhere that requires a bit of shaping. Curved darts are a little trickier to mark and stitch, but provide a beautiful, naturally curved shape.

PLACEMENT MARKS
Placement marks come in a variety of shapes. Circles, dots, squares and triangles are used to mark a spot on the pattern that is referenced in the written instructions. They often indicate a placement point (for a zipper or a pocket, for example), or they might show you where to begin or end stitching. Your instructions will explain what to do.

ADJUSTMENT LINES
Sewing patterns will often have adjustment lines drawn on them, usually labeled "lengthen or shorten here." These lines tell you where it is safe to add or remove fabric without disrupting the overall design. You will often find these lines on the bottom area of bodice patterns, and around the hips or lower on skirts.

BUTTON AND BUTTONHOLE MARKS
Buttonholes might be noted on a pattern by a buttonhole shape, a circle, a circle with a cross or some combination. They will help you determine placement so that buttons are evenly spaced, and also run directly down the center of the placket.

CUTTING LINES
The cutting lines on the pattern are indicated by a series of different outlines, one for each size. The sizes are "nested," meaning they are stacked together, somewhat like a Russian doll. Each size is indicated by a different style of line. Find your size, and cut along that line for each pattern piece.

Anatomy of a Pattern

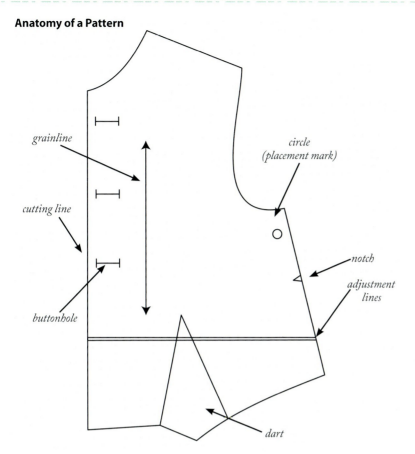

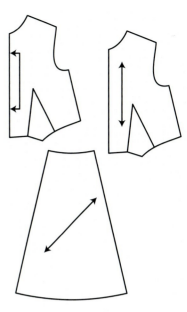

Indications of Grainline

The three illustrations here show three different arrows/grainlines. The illustration at *top left* indicates that the pattern piece should be placed with the left edge against the fabric's foldline. The illustration at *top right* indicates that piece should be placed straight along the fabric's grainline. The *bottom* illustration has an arrow indicating that the piece should be placed on the bias.

Indications of Sizing

Each line style represents a different size for this pattern. For this pattern, I've cut out a size 8. Notice that the pattern markings (the large and small circles) are also printed in multiple sizes. The shears point to a circle for a size 8.

PATTERN + INSTRUCTIONS

Before you start your project, review the instructions and pattern together. The construction symbols should all make sense to you when you begin.

PREPARE YOUR FABRIC

Before cutting into your fabric, you'll need to get it ready with a few simple steps: prewashing, ironing and "trueing up."

PREWASH AND IRON

Washing fabric for the first time can effect it in surprising ways. If you've ever bought a flattering pair of jeans only to have them feel two sizes too small after the first wash, you're undoubtedly aware of the phenomenon known as shrinkage. Along with size changes, washing can also effect the color, texture and drape of fabric, and that can interfere with getting the final product you're after. But unlike off-the-rack clothing, you can minimize these surprises by pretreating your fabric in the exact same way you plan to clean your garment.

Many delicate fabrics, such as silks and rayons, can be washed by hand using a gentle detergent and hung to dry. Rayon shrinks quite a bit, even over multiple washings, so I recommend washing it two or three times before cutting. Silk does not shrink, but it does often change in texture and drape. Sturdier cottons, linens and other substantial fabrics can be washed and dried by machine, and multiple washings will help to soften them up. Wool is usually best left for the dry-cleaner because it can continue to change with each successive washing. Overall, the important thing is that you treat your fabric in the same way you plan to clean it later.

Once the fabric is dry, iron it to remove any wrinkles. Gently iron along the lengthwise grain, running the iron up and down, parallel to the selvages. This will help stretch it into shape after its first washing. You want to get your fabric pretty much into the state it will live in as a garment: washed and ironed and ready to be worn.

Treat Your Fabric Right
You're about to invest quite a bit of thought and time into your very own handmade garment, so why not start your fabric out right? I wash most of my handmade clothing by hand using a gentle, quality detergent with a lovely scent. It's important to prewash your fabric in the same gentle way you plan to treat your garment.

GET IT STRAIGHT

Woven fabrics are created by two sets of threads, one set running lengthwise and one set running crosswise. These are called the lengthwise grain and the crosswise grain. These should ideally be at 90 degrees to one another, and normally, they are. But occasionally, the threads become twisted, or "off grain." This can cause distortion in the fit and drape of your final garment.

The first thing you want to do is make sure that the ends of your fabric have been cut or torn straight across the crosswise grain. Some fabrics tear easily along the crosswise grain, so if you noticed that your fabric was torn off the bolt in the store rather than cut, you're all set. If you're not sure if the ends are exactly straight, it's easy to straighten them yourself. (See right.) This process is often referred to as "trueing up."

Once your ends are straight, fold your fabric in half lengthwise by bringing the selvages together. If your cut or torn ends align, you're ready to start! If they won't align properly, then your fabric is off grain. To fix this, unfold your fabric and, holding it at opposite diagonal corners, give it a firm tug. Do this for both sets of diagonal corners to help the grain straighten out again.

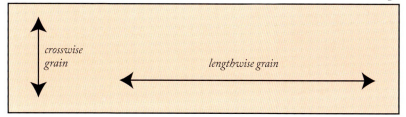

Work With Your Fabric

You want to keep in line with the natural structure of your fabric, not fight against it. That means getting all of the ends parallel to the natural grain of the fabric, both crosswise and lengthwise.

Straightening by Tearing

Some fabrics tear easily on the crosswise grain, and some do not. Try making a small snip right near the end and give it a firm pull to tear it a little bit. If it tears neatly, tear it all the way across and you'll now have a completely straight end to your fabric. Tear the other end in the same way for two perfectly straight edges.

Straightening by Pulling Thread and Cutting

If it won't tear easily, use this second method. Use a pin to pull up one single crosswise thread. Pull it all the way out, from one selvage to the other. Now cut along the line left by the empty space, and you will have a perfectly straight end.

LAY OUT YOUR PATTERN

Your cutting layout will tell you whether fabric should be folded in half, or whether you should lay out a single thickness. If it's folded, simply fold it lengthwise with the front sides together. In either case, lay your fabric so that it's aligned with the edge of your table. Try not to let any excess fabric hang over the edge, where it can pull. Instead, fold it up and set it along the edge of the table, or support it with another table or chair.

When you're ready to cut your fabric, you should first decide how the pieces will be laid out on the fabric. This will largely be determined by your pattern, but you may need to tweak the layout here and there for your particular fabric.

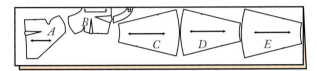

Examine the Pattern's Cutting Layout
Your pattern has diagrams indicating how to lay out your pieces on various widths of fabric, and these are a great place to start. Sometimes you will find that there are slightly more economical ways of laying out your pieces, so feel free to play around a bit. The patternmaker often can't show you the optimal layout for every single size included in the pattern, so testing other layouts can sometimes save a bit of fabric.

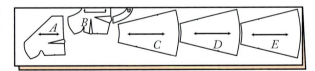

Check for a Nap or One-Way Design
In addition, the type of fabric you use may require a layout other than what's shown. Take a look to see if your fabric looks different when it's held upside down or crossways. Solid fabrics with a nap or pile (like velvet) will look different at these angles, and so will one-way printed designs. If this is the case, you will have to use a one-way layout, in which all the pattern pieces have their top end facing the same direction. Here, I've reversed pieces D, E and A.

PREPARE YOUR PATTERN

Just like your fabric, your pattern should be wrinkle free. Give it a light press with a dry iron to smooth out any wrinkles. Cut your paper pattern carefully, cutting just on the inside of the cutting lines for your size. If you are planning to use the pattern more than once, it can be a good idea to trace the pattern from its original tissue onto sturdier paper. Professional designers and patternmakers often use oak tag, a strong and thick paper similar to a heavy cardstock.

Your local market might have the pattern paper of your dreams. Freezer paper is a sturdy paper with a coating on one side that adheres to fabric when ironed. You can trace your pattern onto it, then iron it right onto your fabric. This makes for highly accurate cutting without the fuss of weights or pins. As a bonus, if your fabric is slippery and difficult to cut, you can fuse the freezer paper to your fabric before cutting to help stabilize the pieces. Then simply cut the paper and fabric at the same time. When you're finished, peel the paper off before sewing. Freezer paper is available from many markets, or you can order it in a variety of widths from packaging suppliers. Be sure to test the freezer paper on a swatch of your fabric to make sure it pulls cleanly away.

LAYING OUT THE PATTERN PIECES

Once you've determined the right layout for your fabric and prepared the pieces, it's time to lay out your pieces.

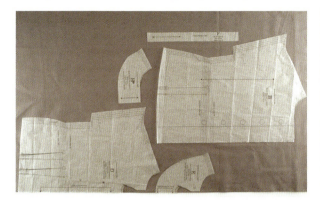

1. Place the pieces that are aligned along the fold first, then set down the larger pieces, and end with the smaller ones. Pattern pieces should be face up, unless your cutting layout tells you otherwise. Fabric should be wrong-side up, so any markings will be on the wrong side.

2. Measure the grainlines.
Check that the arrow on the pattern indicating the grainline is aligned with the grain of your fabric. To do this, measure from each end of the arrow to the fold or to the selvage. If the measurement is the same at both ends of the arrow, then your pattern piece is parallel and aligned correctly. You can use a clear ruler or a measuring tape for longer measurements.

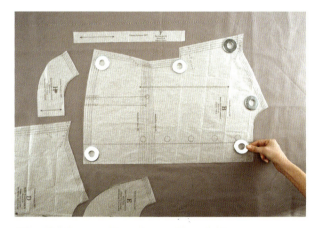

3. Hold your pattern down with weights.
While many people use pins to hold their pattern in place, using too many pins can pinch and distort your fabric, and significantly affect the final shape and fit. Pattern weights are a great alternative. They have the added benefit of making your pieces easy to position and reposition. You can use just about anything small and heavy as a pattern weight, but I'm partial to large metal washers.

SEAM ALLOWANCES

The "seam allowance" is that bit of fabric between the seam line and the cut edge of the fabric. Most home sewing patterns have a standard seam allowance of 5/8" (1.6cm). This distance creates a seam allowance that is strong enough to last, but not so wide that it creates excess bulk in the garment.

However, some seam allowances may be wider or narrower, and these should always be noted on your pattern. Deeply curved areas, for example, can be easier to sew with a smaller seam allowance. Some pattern companies—particularly European companies—use different allowances for their patterns.

LAYING OUT PATTERN PIECES WITH STRIPED OR PLAID FABRIC

Impeccably matched stripes that meet at the seams are a hallmark of a careful, experienced sewer. But they are not at all difficult if you take a little care when cutting. There are two approaches you can take, depending on whether you need the pattern to match on identical/mirror image pieces, or along the seams of completely different pieces.

WORKING WITH IDENTICAL PATTERN PIECES

Often, you will cut two mirror image pattern pieces at once, by folding the fabric in half. To make sure stripes or plaids align, match them up at the selvages and ends of the fabric before cutting.

Align the Fabric's Stripes

When you're cutting two mirror image pieces from one pattern piece, just align the fabric's stripes. In the photo, I am cutting two back pieces for a blouse, the right and left side. Because they meet at the center with buttons, it's important that the stripes match up in the middle. By lining up the stripes all along the selvage before cutting, I know that both pieces have stripes in the same placement, and that they'll meet up at the button placket. This method is easy and perfect for any identical pieces that will be sewn down the center, such as a bodice with a seam down the front.

lines/patterns match at selvage and ends

WORKING WITH DIFFERENT PATTERN PIECES

For different pattern pieces, you'll need to draw a "match stripe." In this example, I want the stripes on the front and back of a bodice to meet perfectly at the shoulder seam.

1. Create a "match point."

In this pattern, the Front and Back Bodice pieces should be laid out on the fold—but then the plaids won't match at the shoulder seams. To address this, lay one pattern piece on the fold. Align the second pattern piece with the first at the shoulder seam, folding each edge back ⅝" (1.6cm) to account for seam allowance. Pick a line on the fabric, and mark a "match point" in the center where the seams meet/where the line meets at the shoulder seam. Whether you use a pen or pin, make sure you mark on both pattern pieces. In this case, I've chosen the edge of a black line for my match point.

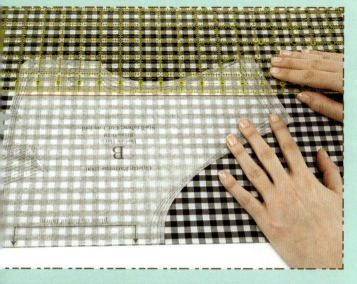

2. **Draw a match line on the first piece.**
Leave the first piece in place along the fold. Using a rotary ruler and marker, trace from the match point along the line in the fabric to the bottom of the pattern piece. Here, I'm tracing along the black line.

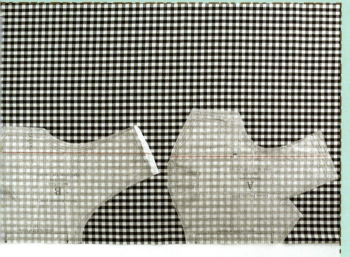

3. **Repeat for the second piece.**
Draw a straight line from the match point to the bottom of the second pattern piece. The line should be parallel to the grainline marked on the pattern piece. For a vertical seam (like a side seam), the line would be 90° to the grainline.

You can see here that if the second pattern piece were cut on the fold, the plaid pattern would not match.

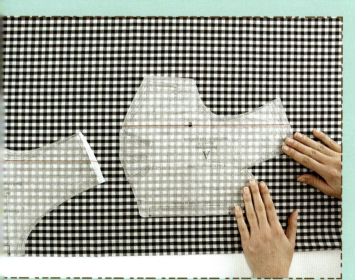

4. **Re-position the second pattern piece.**
Leaving the first pattern piece on the fold, reposition the second piece so that its match line falls along a matching stripe.

At this point, you would cut out the first piece. You would then refold the fabric so that your second pattern piece is positioned on the fold, with the match line on your selected stripe, and cut.

Because the pattern is even, it will match at both shoulder seams when the pieces are unfolded and sewn together.

TRANSFER THE MARKINGS

Transferring all of the construction marks from your pattern will help you immensely as you're creating your garment. The pattern instructions will refer to these marks frequently, providing a vital link between the instructions you read and what you see in front of you when sewing.

When is the best time to mark your pieces? So far, we've talked about getting all of your pattern pieces laid out, with pattern weights holding them in place. If you are going to be using fabric shears to cut your fabric, the best way to get an accurate cut is to first trace the cutting lines onto your fabric, transfer all of the construction marks, then remove the pattern before cutting. If you use a rotary cutter instead of shears, you can cut your pattern first without removing the pattern pieces, then transfer the construction marks.

MARKING TOOLS

The ideal marking tool depends on your fabric and what sort of marks your need to transfer. It's best to have an assortment, because you will likely use them all in your sewing career, and each project may be different. I often use a variety of marking methods within one project. There are no exact rules. You just need a tool that will produce marks that are easy to see, stay put while you're sewing and will disappear from your fabric when you're done.

Marking Tools
These marking tools are widely available and are generally water soluble or easy to remove. Tailor's chalk is wonderful for easy marking, but becomes dull rather quickly, whereas water soluble pens and pencils give a fine line but are sometimes hard, waxy or difficult to see. A chalk liner combines the best of both worlds by releasing a fine line of loose chalk through its tip.

Mark With Pencils, Pens or Chalk
To transfer the markings, push a pin through your pattern and fabric at the point you want to mark. Then just lift the paper pattern and mark the fabric at the exact point the pin is stuck through. Life the fabric slightly and mark the other side before pulling out your pin. This can be tricky if you haven't cut your pieces out yet. In that case, wait until you've cut the pattern before marking the other side.

Mark With Tailor's Tacks

Tailors tacks employ needle and thread to mark certain points on the fabric. First, make a small slit in your paper pattern at the point you wish to mark. Then use a needle and fine thread (I recommend silk or fine cotton) and sew several extremely loose loops at this point, through all layers of your fabric, leaving long thread tails at the ends. Remove the pattern and gently pull apart the two layers of fabric slightly. With your scissors between the two layers, cut the thread loops in the center. You will now have a tack on each piece in the same spot. Because I find that tailor's tacks fall out easily, I often follow them up with chalk or thread tracing.

 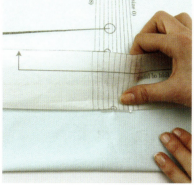 

Mark With Snips

You can use your scissors to mark points that occur along the edges of your pattern pieces, such as match points at notches. Just make a small snip in the seam allowance at these points. (Combining snips at the endpoints with a pin at the tip makes marking dart placement very fast and easy!)

Mark With Pins

Transferring marks doesn't need to be laborious. A quick and easy way to transfer marks is just to insert a pin at marking points, such as circles or dart tips. If you are cutting two layers, be sure to turn your pattern over and mark the opposite side as well. Pins are a very easy way to mark single points, and work well for most fabrics, as long as they're not very loosely woven, which can cause pins to fall out easily.

Mark With Thread Tracing

Tracing marks with thread is a traditional method and extremely useful because it can be done on any fabric and is highly reliable. You can use different colors for different types of markings, and best of all in my book, the tracings show on both sides of the fabric. Again, I recommend a fine silk or cotton thread, as they are less damaging to fabric. Use hand basting stitches to create lines or single marks on your fabric.

CUT YOUR FABRIC

A common mistake among eager sewers is to rush through the cutting, being a little careless with the lines of the pattern. What seems like a small bit of extra fabric on one piece multiplies with all of the other pieces, and pretty soon, your garment is a full size larger than you. Or your pieces don't line up along the seam, so you have to trim a little off here and there, which has a cascading effect. Pretty soon, none of your seams match and sewing becomes more difficult than it needs to be.

Your pattern is like a jigsaw puzzle; the pieces go together in a very specific way. That isn't to say that you can't make changes. In fact, much of the time you should if you want something perfect for you! But any changes you make to the pieces should be thoughtful and intentional, so that they will continue to fit together. Sewing already has so many variables, why make it harder on yourself by introducing guesswork?

STABILIZE TRICKY FABRICS

Some fabrics are notoriously hard to handle when it's time to cut. Light and filmy fabrics, such as chiffon, can shift at the slightest breeze, while slippery fabrics, such as charmuese, seem determined to slide right off the table. What you need is a temporary stabilizer.

One option to keep these tricky beauties in check is a spray stabilizer. You simply spray it onto your entire piece of prewashed fabric and let it dry. The formerly temperamental fabric will become stiff and easy to work with until you wash it again. Spray starch is similar, but has more of a tendency to scorch.

If you're uneasy about spraying anything onto your favorite silks, a second option is to place paper on your cutting table, underneath your fabric. Then, just use your shears to cut right through the paper along with the fabric. Be careful because cutting through paper can dull your shears quickly, so have them sharpened frequently.

50

Fabric Shears Are Versatile

Many sewers use a sharp pair of fabric shears to cut their fabric. Shears are easy to use and versatile, conquering tight corners and angles with ease. They can cut through the bulkiest fabrics without a problem, and can be used for a variety of tasks in the sewing room, such as snipping threads or cutting notches. A good pair of shears, properly maintained, will last you through the years. Whether or not you choose to do most of your cutting with shears, you'll still find them indispensable for general sewing tasks.

Before you cut, trace the pattern and transfer all the marks, as well as the outline of the pattern. Cut your fabric right along the traced edge. Use long, full strokes rather than short and choppy ones whenever possible. When you get to tighter curves or angles, use shorter strokes.

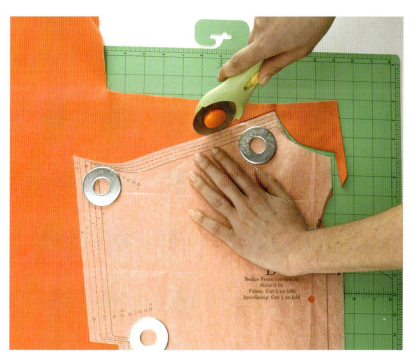

Rotary Cutters Are Efficient

Rotary cutters have great benefits in terms of speed and efficiency. The round blade rolls along the fabric as it cuts without lifting the fabric from the cutting surface. This means you can cut with the paper pattern on your fabric, without tracing the lines onto your fabric, and still get a precise cut. Once you've gotten the hang of it, you can get your cutting done in about half the time. The downside to being so speedy is that it's easy to make mistakes and easy to cut your fingers, so be careful. You'll need to purchase a cutting mat to protect the surface underneath. Invest in a large one so there's no need to upgrade later.

Project

MERINGUE SKIRT

*E*ven with its pretty scalloped hem, this skirt has a simple and straightforward construction, making it a great choice for practicing working with a pattern. It has a simple darted fit and sits just slightly below the natural waist. You can use it to experiment with new marking techniques you may not have tried before, such as tailor's tacks, or try out the freezer paper tip for cutting your pattern pieces. Practice taking your time and cutting carefully around the curves. We'll also create a small paper template to help you mark the scalloped stitching line at the hem. Once you've finished that lovely hem, you'll most certainly see how careful and accurate marking can make sewing less frustrating.

We'll also cover my preferred technique for attaching a facing to a zipper. For this skirt, we'll be using an invisible zipper, which is perhaps the easiest zipper to install. For help with putting the zipper in, review the page 23.

Start by using the steps we covered in this chapter to cut out your pattern and transfer the markings, then move into the instructions to put your skirt together.

(The blouse in this photo is the Sencha pattern, published by Colette Patterns.)

TOOLS

sewing shears (or rotary cutter and mat)
pattern weights
pins
hand sewing needle
marking pen or chalk
French curve ruler
paper (for template)
paper scissors (for template)
invisible zipper presser foot
bamboo point turner/presser (optional)
pinking shears (optional)

SUPPLIES

fabric (see Fabric Suggestions and Fabric Required table)
lightweight fusible interfacing (see Fabric Required table)
thread
9" (22.9cm) invisible zipper
one small hook and eye closure
piece of paper for making a template

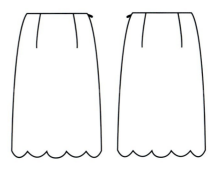

SKILLS CHECKLIST

* *Preparing your fabric (pp. 42–43)*
* *Laying out your pattern (pp. 44–45)*
* *Transferring the markings (pp. 48–49)*
* *Cutting out your pattern (pp. 50–51)*
* *Sewing darts (pp. 20–21)*
* *Pressing a seam (p. 18)*
* *Sewing an invisible zipper (p23)*
* *Attaching a facing to a zipper (p. 22)*
* *Sewing a catchstitch by hand (p. 17)*

FABRIC SUGGESTIONS

Choose a stiff fabric that holds its shape well, in order to keep the scallops crisp and easy to sew. Medium-weight fabrics, such as silk twill, dupioni, cotton pique, brocade, taffeta or poplin are good choices. Lighter home décor fabrics work well for this skirt, too.

FABRIC REQUIRED (YARDS AND METERS):

To find your size, check the size chart at the end of the book.

	0	2	4	6	8	10	12	14	16	18
FABRIC, 45" (115 CM)	2⅛ yards (1.9m)	2⅛ yards (1.9 m)	2¼ yards (2 m)	2¼ yards (2 m)	2¼ yards (2 m)	2⅓ yards (2.1 m)	2⅓ yards (2.1 m)	2⅓ yards (2.1 m)	2⅓ yards (2.1 m)	2⅓ yards (2.1 m)
FABRIC, 60" (150 CM)	2⅛ yards (1.9 m)	2⅛ yards (1.9 m)	2¼ yards (2 m)	2¼ yards (2 m)	2¼ yards (2 m)	2⅓ yards (2.1 m)	2⅓ yards (2.1 m)	2⅓ yards (2.1 m)	2⅓ yards (2.1 m)	2⅓ yards (2.1 m)
NONWOVEN FUSIBLE INTERFACING, 20" (50 CM)	¾ yard (0.7 m)	¾ yard (0.7 m)	¾ yard (0.7 m)	¾ yard (0.7 m)	¾ yard (0.7 m)	¾ yard (0.7 m)	¾ yard (0.7 m)	¾ yard (0.7 m)	¾ yard (0.7 m)	¾ yard (0.7 m)

FINISHED GARMENT MEASUREMENTS (INCHES):

	0	2	4	6	8	10	12	14	16	18
SKIRT LENGTH*	22½" (57 cm)	22¾" (58 cm)	23" (58 cm)	23¼" (59 cm)	23½" (60 cm)	23¾" (60 cm)	24" (61 cm)	24¼" (62 cm)	24½" (62 cm)	24¾" (63 cm)
HEM WIDTH	44" (112 cm)	45" (114 cm)	46" (117 cm)	47" (119 cm)	48" (122 cm)	49½" (126 cm)	51" (129 cm)	53" (135 cm)	55" (140 cm)	57" (145 cm)
WAIST	26½" (67 cm)	27½" (70 cm)	28½" (72 cm)	29½" (75 cm)	30½" (77 cm)	32" (81 cm)	33½" (85 cm)	35½" (90 cm)	37½" (95 cm)	39½" (100 cm)
HIP	38" (97 cm)	39" (99 cm)	40" (102 cm)	41" (104 cm)	42" (107 cm)	43½" (110 cm)	45" (114 cm)	47" (119 cm)	49" (124 cm)	51" (130 cm)

* Skirt length is measured from your natural waist to the hem.

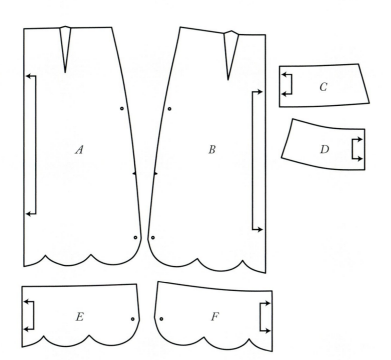

PATTERN INVENTORY

A - Skirt Front
B - Skirt Back
C - Front Waist Facing
D - Back Waist Facing
E - Front Hem Facing
F - Back Hem Facing

All pieces include ⅝" (1.6 cm) seam allowance.

CUTTING LAYOUT

Fabric most frequently comes in widths of 45" (115 cm) or 60" (152 cm), but widths do vary. Your cutting layout may also need to change for a napped or one-way fabric (see page 44 for details), or you may need a different layout for matching stripes or plaids (see pages 46–47).

MAIN FABRIC, 45" (115 CM) OR 60" (152 CM):

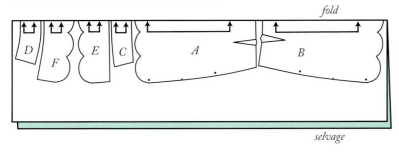

INTERFACING, 20" (50 CM), FOLD CROSSWISE:

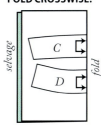

INSTRUCTIONS

MARK YOUR PIECES

1. Begin by following the guidelines in this chapter to prepare your fabric, lay out your pattern, transfer the markings and cut your fabric.

2. To help you sew the curves evenly, mark the stitching line for the hem on the facing pieces. To do this, create a template. Templates can help you draw guidelines when you need to stitch more complicated shapes. Trace the edge of one of the hem curves onto a separate sheet of paper. Measure ⅝" (1.6 cm) in from several points along the curve, then connect these lines with a curve, using a French curve ruler to draw the curve accurately. Cut your paper template along this new line. (Figure 1) You will use this template on a single curve to trace all the curves that form the stitching line for the scallops.

3. On Front HemFacing (E) and Back Hem Facing (F), use your new curve template to trace a seamline with a marking pen or chalk, beginning and ending at the small circles on each side of the wrong side of the fabric. (Figure 2)

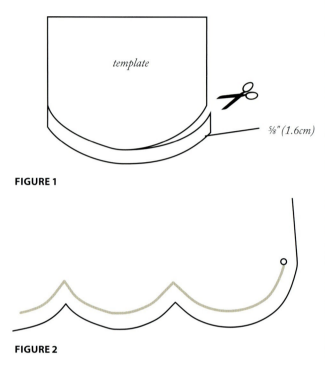

FIGURE 1

FIGURE 2

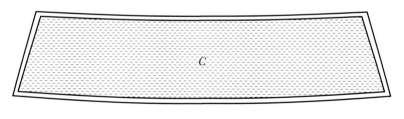

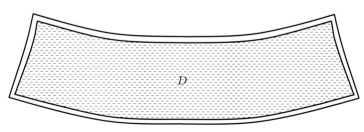

APPLY INTERFACING

1. Apply fusible interfacing to the wrong side of Front Waist Facing (C) and Back Waist Facing (D), following the manufacturer's instructions for your interfacing. (Figure 3)

FIGURE 3

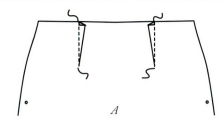
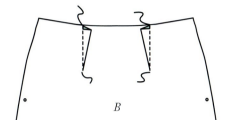

SEW DARTS

1. On Skirt Front (A) and Skirt Back (B), bring the legs of each dart together and pin. Stitch darts from the edges toward the points and tie off the ends.

2. Press darts toward the center on both the front and back. (Figure 4)

FIGURE 4

SEW SIDE SEAMS

1. With right sides together, Stitch Skirt Front (A) to Skirt Back (B) at what will be the right side seam. Press the seam open and finish the raw edges. (Figure 5)

2. With right sides together, stitch Front Waist Facing (C) to Back Waist Facing (D) at what will be the right side seam. Press the seam open. Note that, with the pieces wrong side out, the left side seam of the facing will appear to be on the opposite side when compared to the skirt itself. That is because the facing will sit with the right side toward your body, whereas the skirt will have the right side facing outward. (Figure 6) Before continuing, take a look at figures 5 and 6 and make sure your side seams appear as shown in the diagrams.

3. With right sides together, stitch Front Hem Facing (E) to Back Hem Facing (F) at the side seams, starting at the top and ending at the circle. Press the seams open. (Figure 7)

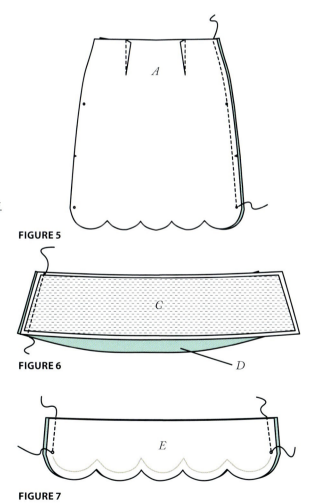

FIGURE 5

FIGURE 6

FIGURE 7

57

INSERT ZIPPER

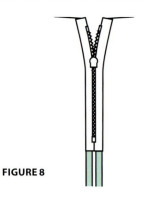

FIGURE 8

1. Finish the raw edges of the side seam, on the side where the zipper will be sewn. It's easier to finish these edges before putting in the zipper. See chapter six to learn more about seam finishes.

2. Using an invisible zipper foot on your sewing machine, sew the invisible zipper into the left side seam above the large circle. For detailed instructions, see page 23. (If you choose to add a lining, see pages 144-145.)

3. Stitch the left side seam closed below the zipper, between the large circle at the bottom of the zipper and the small circle near the hem. Press the seam open. (Figure 8)

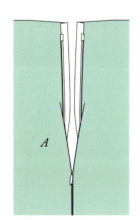

FIGURE 9

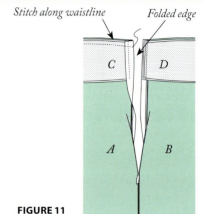

FIGURE 10   **FIGURE 11**

SEW WAIST FACING

1. Finish the lower edge of the waist facing. To do this without adding bulk, you might choose to pink the edge, sew a zigzag stitch along it, or sew lace hem tape to it. (See chapter six to learn more about seam finishes.)

2. Now that you have the zipper installed, you're going to sew the facing in while attaching it to the zipper, for a very clean finish. To begin, hold your skirt with the right side facing you. At the top of the zipper opening, fold the seam allowance and zipper out so that the back of the zipper is facing up, toward you. (Figure 9)

3. With right sides together, place the waist facing pieces on top of the skirt, aligning all of the edges using a zipper foot. Stitch the facing in place at the opening edges, stitching close to the zipper teeth. You will be stitching within the seam allowance. (Figure 10)

4. Fold the opening edges toward you again, along the zipper. The zipper should now be between the seam allowance and the wrong side of the facing. Do this on both sides of the opening and pin in place.

5. Stitch the facing to the skirt along the waistline (Figure 11), from one opening edge all the way to the other. Trim the seam and clip the corners. Understitch the waistline seam allowance as far as possible, stopping when you get within a few inches of the zipper. Turn the facing to the inside of the skirt and press. (See page 22 for detailed instructions on installing facings.) Sew a single hook and eye closure above the zipper.

SEW HEM FACING

1. Finish the upper edge of the hem facing. To do this without adding bulk, you might choose to pink the edge, sew a zigzag stitch along it or sew lace hem tape to it. See chapter six to learn more about seam finishes.

2. With right sides together, pin the hem facing to the skirt, aligning the raw edges.

3. Stitch the hem facing to the skirt, stitching carefully along the stitching line that you marked earlier, and pivoting at the inner points of each scallop. (Figure 12)

4. Trim and grade the hem seam to a scant ¼" (6 mm). Notch the outer curves all along the seam. Cut a notch at each inner point to remove the excess fabric there. (Figure 13)

5. Turn the facing to the inside. Press, using the bamboo point turner to help push out the seam from the inside as you press. If you don't have a point turner, you can also use a knitting needle to push out seams.

6. Use a catchstitch to hand stitch the upper facing edge to the inside of the skirt in order to secure it in place. See page 17 for detailed instructions on the catchstitch.

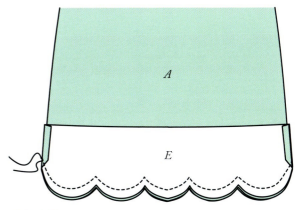

FIGURE 12

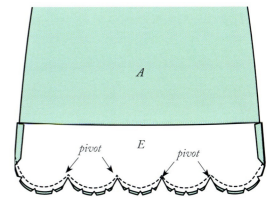

FIGURE 13

GRADING SEAMS

When you have multiple layers of seam allowance within a seam, such as when you sew in a facing like this, you risk bulky seams. To help prevent this, use a simple technique called seam grading. First trim the entire seam allowance by half. Then trim the side of the seam allowance that will lay closest to your body in half again. This staggers the layers of fabric to make the seam smooth.

Chapter Four
A FANTASTIC FIT

Many of us decide to take up sewing because we want clothes that are just right for us. We want them to be in the styles we like, in the colors and fabrics that excite us, and crafted just for our bodies. We dream of having a closet full of clothes that express our creativity and also make us look great. And we care enough about it to invest time in learning the variety of skills it takes to assemble cloth and thread into the garments we dream of.

A big part of this dream is having clothing that works with our bodies. The problem is that a pattern that comes straight off the shelf will never have the custom fit that we desire. Sewing patterns are designed to be sewn by thousands of women around the world and so, just like off the rack clothing, they are made for one average body type. They simply cannot account for the huge number of bodily variations that occur, even within a single size! The chances of a pattern fitting you perfectly right off the shelf are slim.

The good news is that with a little patience and knowledge, you can have clothing that works with your body in a way that nothing store-bought ever could. You have the chance to make fully customized clothing, which is something few people who don't sew can afford. It isn't always fast or easy, but you will learn a lot about your body and the way fabric can be shaped around it. You'll end up with clothing you like to wear, and you will be much more confident in your sewing ability than someone who must rely on the elusive perfect store-bought pattern.

WHAT IS A GOOD FIT?

When something fits well, you feel good in it. It glides over your body, neither bunching up nor pulling or straining. It is comfortable. In fact, a good fit is less noticeable than a bad fit, because you don't have to think about the way your clothes are hanging, and you don't have to feel self-conscious about the relationship of your clothes to your body. In some ways, the idea of a good fit is subjective, because it has to do with what makes you feel comfortable. Some people find a loose fit to be right for them, and others like their clothes to be very fitted.

But the bottom line is that a good fit takes into account the shape of your body and conforms around it. Even a very loose-fitting dress should hang comfortably without sagging or bunching up, and a close-fitting dress shouldn't pull or strain. The trick is to eliminate any of these fitting problems by noticing them and fixing them before you sew your garment. That's a process that takes time and a bit of practice.

Fitting is a skill, and like most skills worth acquiring, it takes a little time to master. It's partially about learning the right techniques, and it's partially about training your eye.

The better something fits, the more people will see the person wearing the clothes rather than focusing on the clothes themselves. Not only does a good fit look elegant, but it allows you to better express yourself through the clothes you make. You'll feel better in your handmade clothing and more satisfied with your sewing.

I think there are two main obstacles to getting a good fit when you sew. The first is that, initially, it seems complicated. There are many potential fitting issues and alterations, and figuring out what you need seems intimidating. This is mostly a matter of practice and experience, but it doesn't take very long to figure out. Once you've really examined a pattern in relation to your body, you will find yourself understanding your body better and using the same techniques over and over to get the result you want.

The second obstacle is time. Sometimes we get so excited about a project, we can't wait to finish and wear it. But a good fit requires an investment of time, and that investment will pay off in the form of a garment that you actually love and want to wear. For a really lovely garment, you should expect to spend as much time on fitting as you do sewing. Think of yourself as a custom clothier, because that's exactly what you are. You are making something special and unique to you.

Some people enjoy the fitting process and some find it a burden. If you find it tiresome to fit a pattern every time you sew, why not work with just a few patterns that you love and have perfected, rather than trying a new pattern every time? There's nothing wrong with having a small library of custom fitted patterns, and you may end up much happier with the results. I believe most sewers would be happier with a few patterns in the styles they love than a huge hit-or-miss collection. I love to make a dress that fits well multiple times, varying the fabric and adding details or embellishments. If you take the guesswork out of sewing, I promise there will be fewer tears in the sewing room.

Too Tight

Even if something is meant to be tight, it shouldn't strain against the body and produce these tight wrinkles. Here, you can see that the dress is straining across the bust, around the rib cage and a bit near the armpit.

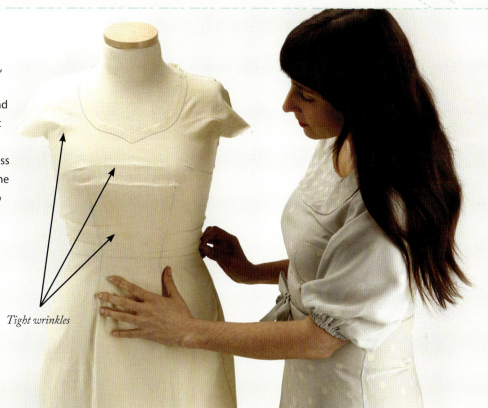

Tight wrinkles

Too Loose

On the other hand, a loose garment shouldn't sag or gape, which produces loose wrinkles. Here, you see loose, vertical wrinkles from the bust, below the waist and around the armholes.

Loose wrinkles

EASE

To understand the basics of fit, we'll start with the concept of ease. *Ease* is quite simply the difference between your body's measurements and the measurements of your garment. A garment in a nonstretch fabric with no ease would be absolutely skin tight, with no room to move around, breathe normally or remain comfortable.

There are two types of ease. Wearing ease is the small amount of ease needed for movement and comfort. For a very close fitting garment, this might be 2" (5.1 cm) in the bust, ½" (1.3 cm) in the waist and 2" (5.1 cm) at the hips.

The other type of ease is design ease. This is additional ease added by the designer to achieve a certain look or effect. For example, think of a blousey top such as a peasant blouse. It has design ease added around the bodice to make it look billowy and less form fitting than a basic shell. Typically, softer, lighter and more flowing fabrics look better with more ease than crisp fabrics.

When you are sewing from a pattern, you may want to know how much ease the designer has intended a garment to have. With experience, you'll find the amount of ease you prefer in various styles and fabrics.

The ease is easy to calculate. Pattern companies list the finished garment measurement on their packaging, so all you need to do is subtract the standard body measurements for that size from the garment measurements. Now you know how much ease is supposed to be in each area. Of course, pattern companies can't list every finished measurement, so if you can't find one, just measure the pattern pieces themselves, making sure that you subtract the seam allowances. You'll find that different pattern companies design for different amounts of ease.

Less Ease
This dress has a small amount of wearing ease, with little added design ease, for a very close-fitting result. It works well because the fabric is crisp and sturdy, and the design is tailored.

More Ease
In contrast, this dress is meant to be very loose. The designer has added design ease to give a specific look. Instead of a tailored look, it has soft gathers and is made in a very lightweight and flowing fabric.

DARTS AND FULLNESS

The human body is a complex shape, particularly when you think about all the curves of the female form. Luckily, there is a very simple solution for accommodating those curves: the dart.

Think about a female body as a geometric shape. Like any three-dimensional shape, it has height, depth and width. But unlike a simple geometric shape, such as a cylinder, there are bulges and curves all over the place. *Darts* and *seams* work together to help you sculpt flat pieces of fabric around that wonderfully complex and curvy form.

I'll illustrate how darts shape fabric with an example: Imagine that you are making a very simple tank top. You cut a piece of fabric into the simplest possible shape for a tank top. It's basically a cylinder of fabric with holes for the arms and head. The front of the tank top is shown (above right), and because it's so simple and boxy, it measures 18" (45.7 cm) across the bust, and 18" (45.7 cm) across the waist.

But you want this tank top to be fitted. What you want to do is remove some of that ease at the waist so that the bust remains the same size, but the waist is reduced to only 15" (38.1 cm) across. Darts are the answer to this problem. By adding two 1½" (3.8cm) darts at the waist, you can keep the bust measurement the same while reducing the size of the waist to 15" (38.1 cm) across. This method of removing ease to accommodate curves is known as dart control, and it is one of the building blocks of clothing design.

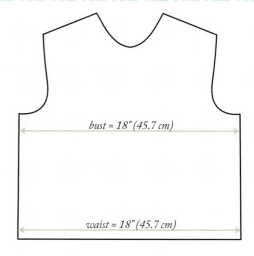

Unshaped Tank Top
This very simple shape hangs straight down from the bust like a sack. The bust and waist measure the same across. You can imagine how boxy it would look on a person.

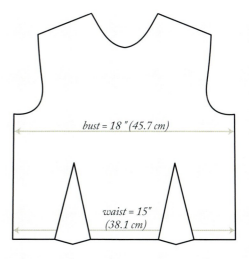

Shaped Tank Top
When the darts are sewn, you will be essentially removing those two wedges of fabric. The waist will become smaller and the front of the tank top will be fitted to the front curves of the body.

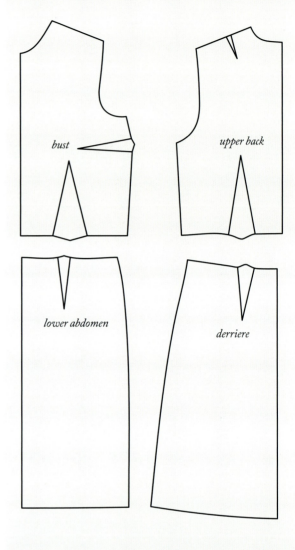

Curves of the Female Form

In this photo, you can clearly see the major curves of the female body: bust, lower abdomen, upper back and derriere. Each of these curves has a high point, known as the apex. Notice how the darts on the dress seem to point toward some of these curves.

How Pattern Pieces Accommodate Curves

Now take a look at the pattern pieces for a typical, fitted dress. Note that this is a slightly different dress than the one shown in the photo. You might notice that each dart corresponds to one of those curves, and that the tip of each dart points to an apex. The wider a dart is, the more fullness can be accommodated at the apex, so you will also notice that the biggest curves (the bust and derriere) have the widest darts. Designers can add darts, remove darts or rotate them around to achieve different looks.

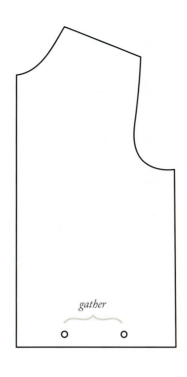

Dart Alternatives

What about designs that have no darts at all? Even those probably use the same principles of dart control. There are many ways to control fullness, such as gathering, tucks, pintucks or pleats. They work in much the same way, by removing a certain amount of fabric when they're stitched. So once a pattern is created using darts, the darts can be converted into one of these other design details very easily. In this example, I've changed a dart into a gather. This will still take away some fabric and provide shaping, but the effect will be much softer and billowy compared to the dart.

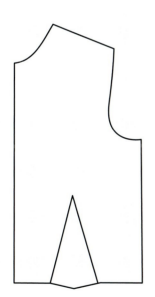 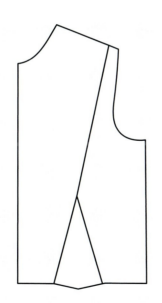 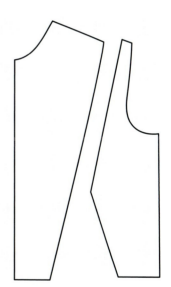

A Dart to a Seam

A dart can even be converted into a seam. Take a look at this pattern example. It starts out with a dart at the waistline. But if we draw a line from the apex of the dart up to the shoulder, then cut along that line, we now have two separate pattern pieces. If we sewed them back together along the seam we've just created, the effect would be the same as the dart. This is how we get a princess seamed bodice, for example. Princess seams like this can give an even more tailored, fitted effect than darts. They are often used in the design of coats and jackets.

HOW TO FIT

The process of truly fitting a garment to your body takes time. Some sewers prefer to rush through it, take shortcuts or do no fitting at all. I know how tempting this is, especially when you're excited about finishing and wearing something. But cutting these kinds of corners in making your own clothing can really end up being a false economy. Sure, it seems to save you time in the short term, but if you end up spending hours sewing something that you won't wear because of a poor fit, you've wasted more time than you've saved. Plus, you'll end up disappointed and frustrated.

Instead, I invite you to think of your sewing room as your own personal custom dressmaking studio. You are both the talented craftsperson making the clothes, and the client who must be happy wearing them. Take your time, and make something beautiful for yourself!

STEPS TO A BEAUTIFUL FIT

1. MEASURE
Take accurate measurements and choose your size.

2. TRACE
Trace the tissue pattern onto paper for easy adjustments.

3. MAKE A MUSLIN
Mock up the garment in inexpensive fabric.

4. ADJUST MUSLIN
Tweak the mock up.

5. ALTER THE PATTERN
Transfer the changes to the paper pattern.

Repeat steps 3-5 as necessary.

Sound simple? It really is. It just requires a little patience and a few techniques.

TISSUE FITTING

Some teachers and books recommend tissue fitting instead of spending time on muslins. Tissue fitting is the process of pinning or taping together the tissue paper pattern and trying it on, rather than cutting and sewing a muslin. It is certainly faster, and may be able to help you spot certain fitting problems before you sew, but there are significant drawbacks. Since the pieces of a pattern are usually mirrored, you will only be able to put together half the garment, which makes it very difficult to get an exact fit. And tissue paper will never fit the way fabric fits, making it even more challenging. I recommend taking just a little more time to work with a sewn garment in real fabric. If you really need to save time, do a partial muslin by testing out just the most fitted parts.

Custom Fitting
Treat yourself to custom-made clothing by customizing the fit before you cut your fabric.

DRESS FORMS

A dress form is a very convenient tool when you're trying to fit a garment. It allows you to see your garment on a body from all angles and make adjustments without the aid of a friend.

But keep in mind that a dress form may not duplicate all the little quirks of your own body. A dress form also doesn't move, and clothes can look and feel very different on a moving body. So whether or not you use one, it's still a good idea to try on garments as you're fitting them. If you can't find a dress form with exactly your size (which is pretty likely), you can buy one with some measurements that are slightly smaller, and pad them out until they are the same as yours. Simply add a bit of quilt batting to the area, then wrap the area with a stretchy knit fabric. You can even add an old bra stuffed with batting to fill out the bust.

STEP 1: MEASURE

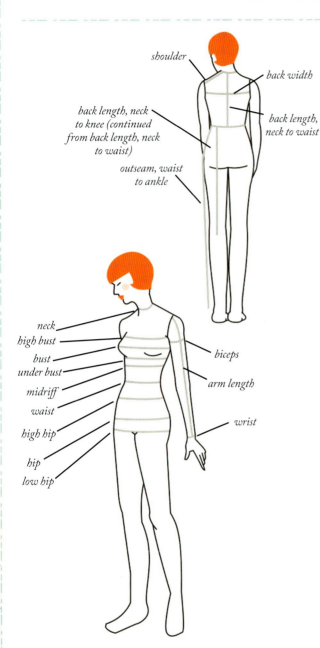

The first step in fitting is getting your measurements down. Keep a list of your measurements on hand in your sewing room, and be sure to jot down the date you took them.

TAKE MEASUREMENTS

It's hard to overestimate the importance of accurate measurements for sewing. Unfortunately, many women are fearful about knowing their real measurements. It may sound silly, but I've heard plenty of women admit that they'd rather guess at their size than know the truth and work with it. Being ashamed of your body's shape is unnecessary at best. At worst, at least in terms of sewing, it undermines your hard work and your self-confidence in wearing your own creations. Don't fret over the numbers. Focus on what's really important, making the things that make you happy.

There are a great number of measurements that may come in handy, depending on the types of things you choose to sew. Generally, the most common measurements you need will be bust, waist, hip, shoulder width and back length.

If possible, have a friend help you when taking measurements because it can be difficult to take some of these measurements by yourself. Wear only the undergarments you will wear under your clothing, and if you plan to wear some special foundation garment under a certain garment (such as a strapless bra, bustier or control slip) remeasure yourself with that on. Stand or sit naturally when you are being measured, and be sure not to suck in your belly or stand more upright than you normally do.

The Basic Measurements
These figures show most of the measurements you may need in sewing. It's a good idea to gather these and record them for later. Be sure to update periodically, especially if your body goes through noticeable changes.

CHOOSE YOUR SIZE

Once you have your measurements at hand, use them to determine the pattern size you need. Check the size chart on the pattern of your choice to find the closest size for you. For the patterns in this book, check the size chart on page 173.

Your measurements may be slightly off in one area from the size chart. For example, your hips might be a little larger than the size you are closest to. Different measurements are important for different types of clothing, so try to determine what the most important measurements are for what you're about to sew. For most skirts and pants, you will want to look at both the waist and hip and go with the larger of the two. For dresses and tops, you will usually go by bust size and adjust the rest of the garment to fit.

If the difference is a size or greater, you may want to cut a different size in each area. Many women with larger hips find this necessary. Multisized patterns make this quite easy. Just mark the bust and the hip lines, then use a curved ruler to gently grade between the sizes.

The large pattern companies have the same sizing, and you may notice that it's significantly different from off-the-rack clothing. Your size number will be larger than the garments you buy. These large pattern companies update their sizing very infrequently, which can be both positive and negative. On the positive side, the sizes are consistent. But on the other hand, the sizes have not kept up with women's changing bodies through the decades. Smaller pattern companies, such as Colette Patterns, have their own signature sizing and fit that is often more specific to the customer type, or closer to modern bodies.

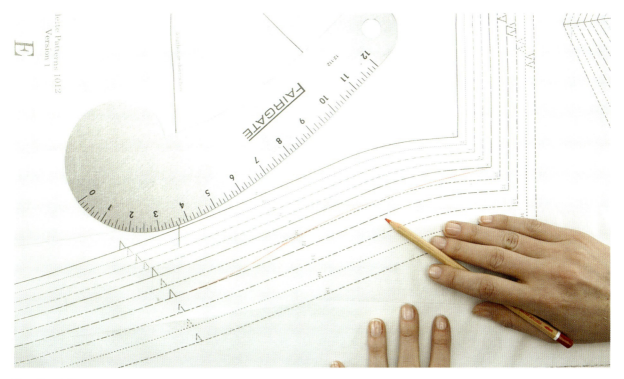

Grading a Curve
Here, I've graded the cutting line from a size 8 at the waist to a size 12 in the hips. The shape of the French curve helps in mimicking the curve of the dress shape for a natural transition.

STEP 2: TRACE

Most sewing patterns come printed on very thin tissue paper, which does not always hold up well over time. Because you are planning to make changes to the pattern in order to fit it to your body, you risk damaging the pattern even more as you cut and tape pieces together. I recommend tracing your pattern pieces onto heavier paper, both to preserve the pattern and to make changes much easier as you go through your fitting. You can even make your own notes on the pattern for future sewing.

You can buy rolls of bond paper to keep on hand, which are available at many art supply or drafting supply stores. Or you can look for inexpensive rolls of wrapping paper, which are wide enough to handle the great majority of sewing patterns. Freezer paper is a great choice as well. As mentioned in chapter three, it has a light coating on one side that causes it to adhere to fabric when ironed, making accurate cutting very easy later on.

Cut out your tissue paper pattern pieces, and make sure they are wrinkle-free. If they seem a bit crumpled, give them a light press with a dry iron. Lay the pieces on your sturdier paper, and trace around all of the cutting lines. Transfer all of the markings for your chosen size onto your new pattern.

Trace Onto Sturdier Paper

Make your own personal pattern by tracing the pieces onto sturdier paper. Label the pieces with the pattern name, pattern piece indicator (such as letter) and size. Dating the pieces can be helpful, too.

STEP 3: MAKE A MUSLIN

Now it's time to create your first draft. This mock-up of your garment is referred to as a muslin, because of the inexpensive muslin fabric from which it's often made. But muslin is not the only choice for your test garment. The most important thing is that your test garment is made in a similar weight and drape to your final project, because these things can have a tremendous effect on the final fit. Gingham is a great choice for many garments, because the checks reveal how the grain of the fabric is falling at a quick glance. I buy gingham by the bolt. You can also collect vintage bed sheets in soft cotton from secondhand stores, or collect fabrics from the sale bins at your local fabric store. It's helpful to keep a stockpile of various fabrics around just for testing things out.

Cut your garment out of your muslin fabric, just as you will the final garment. Transfer all the markings to your fabric with a marker. If a piece is cut on the fold, mark the center line. You can usually omit the facings, lining or any decorative pieces unless there is something you specifically want to try with them. Right now, your focus should be on getting the fit right. Follow the pattern instructions to sew your muslin together. You can skip hemming and leave out the closures, such as zippers or buttons. If you need to save time, you can do a partial muslin by only testing the most fitted portions of a garment, which is often the bodice.

Fitting Help
A friend can help you make adjustments that are difficult to see or reach on your own.

WEARABLE MUSLINS

Many fabrics are suitable for making test garments, but the important thing is to try and match the weight and drape of your real fabric to get a really accurate idea of fit. A "wearable muslin" is a first draft made from a nicer fabric that can be worn when complete. If you find that your muslin only needs small adjustments, a wearable muslin can give you a great preview of the final garment. You can wear it for a day and get a clear idea of fit and comfort. The potential downside is that the wearable muslin may have imperfections, and you must be prepared to end up scrapping it if it needs serious pattern adjustment. Don't use a precious fabric, and be realistic about the potential problems with any first draft.

STEP 4: ADJUST THE MUSLIN

When something fits properly, it is comfortable and lays smoothly over the body. A poor fit will cause wrinkles to appear when you're standing still, either from strain or sagging. Noticing and eliminating these fitting wrinkles is the real key to eliminating fit problems. They aren't hard to spot once you know what to look for.

There are two types of fitting wrinkles. Tight wrinkles are the result of strain on a particular area and indicate that you need to add more fabric. Loose wrinkles are the result of sagging and mean that there is too much fabric in a particular area so that it is not conforming to the body the way it should. In this case, you need to remove some fabric.

Tight Horizontal Wrinkles
Tight horizontal wrinkles mean that there is not enough width in a particular area. You will need to add ease to make the piece wider.

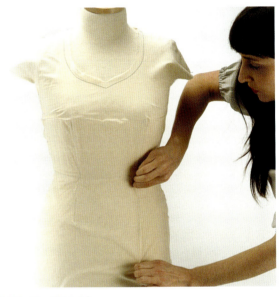

Tight Vertical Wrinkles
Tight vertical wrinkles mean that there is not enough length in an area. You will need to add ease to make the area longer.

Tight Diagonal Wrinkles

Tight diagonal wrinkles mean that there is not enough fabric to go around a curve. You will need to add fullness at the curve, making that area both longer and wider. Here you can see tight wrinkles pointing toward the bust, indicating not enough fullness there.

Loose Horizontal Wrinkles

Loose horizontal wrinkles mean that there is too much length in an area. You will need to eliminate some ease to make the area shorter.

Loose Vertical Wrinkles

Loose vertical wrinkles mean that there is too much width in an area. You will need to eliminate some ease to make the area narrower.

Loose Diagonal Wrinkles

Loose diagonal wrinkles mean that there is too much fabric for the size of a curve. You will need to remove fullness at the curve, making that area both shorter and narrower. Here there is too much fullness around the bust area.

ADJUSTING THE MUSLIN

To get rid of wrinkles, make some changes directly to your muslin. You want to add or subtract fabric where you need it. You don't need to worry yet about exactly how you'll alter the pattern. Instead, just try to figure out where you need extra fabric or less fabric, and how much. Does the bust need an extra inch of room? Does the waist need to be a couple inches smaller? Do you need a little more space at the front of your tummy? These are the alterations you'll bring back to the pattern pieces to make them work for you.

MUSLIN TOO TIGHT

If an area is too small, use your shears to slash it open and make more room. You can pin fabric scraps behind the opening to get it to the size you want

MUSLIN TOO LOOSE

To adjust for looseness, pinch out any excess fullness. Use pins to hold the fold of fabric in place, and re-examine the fit. Once you've added or eliminated the ease you need, measure to see how much you've changed. Mark your changes directly on the muslin, using a different color marker from the other markings. I like to use red for corrections.

STEP 5: ALTER THE PATTERN

Now you know how much fabric you need to add or subtract in certain areas. You will be able to mark those changes directly on the pattern pieces and then alter the pattern pieces to give you the best fit.

In the following pages, we'll cover some of the most common alterations, including simple slash alterations, pivot alterations and fullness alterations. Fitting is a large topic, and there are dozens of possible alterations. We don't have room here to address every fitting challenge, but I hope to give you an introduction to the concepts, along with some solutions to very common fit problems. These are shown on the simplest dress shapes, but you'll find the same alterations applicable to many patterns you use. For more complete instruction on the variety of alterations you can do, I highly recommend picking up a good reference book specifically on fitting. *The Perfect Fit: A Classic Guide to Altering Patterns* provides a wonderful background. For a truly comprehensive fitting manual, check out *Fitting and Pattern Alteration* by Liechty, Rasband and Pottberg-Steineckert.

COMMON ALTERATIONS

BUST:
Full bust | Small bust
High bust | Low bust

BACK:
Narrow back | Broad back
Rounded upper back
Flat back | Sway back

ARM:
Large biceps
Large arm | Small arm

SHOULDERS:
Sloping shoulders
Square shoulders Narrow shoulders
Broad shoulders
Round shoulders

TORSO:
Short-waisted | Long-waisted
Broad chest | Narrow chest
Large rib cage

DERRIERE:
Protruding Derriere
Flat Derriere

LOWER ABDOMEN AND HIPS:
Protruding lower abdomen
Protruding hip bones
Wide hips | Narrow hips

TYPES OF ALTERATIONS

There are several types of alterations that you can do, depending on where you need to make a change. Each of them involves slashing the pattern along a line (or a few lines), then spreading or overlapping them in a specific way to add or remove ease. Spreading the pieces will add more ease to an area, and overlapping will remove some.

SLASH ALTERATION

The first type I will call a simple slash alteration. This involves slashing the pattern piece all the way through, either vertically or horizontally, and simply spreading or overlapping the pieces, keeping the pieces parallel along the slash. In this way, you can make a garment longer or shorter, or add width all the way through from top to bottom.

PIVOT ALTERATION

Let's say you need to add or remove fabric in a specific area along a seam. For example, you may want to add width for larger hips, but you don't want to add fabric at the waist. In this case, you will slash the pattern up to a point on the seamline. Pivot the pieces along this point to add or remove ease where you need it. Because you are pivoting at the seam and not the cutting edge, you will have a little hinge within the seam allowance that you will need to either fold in or clip.

FULLNESS ALTERATION

Last, we have a fullness alteration. This type of alteration is slightly more complex at first glance. Imagine that you want to add some fabric at the bust. How do you accomplish this without also adding width at the waist and shoulders, or length at the side seams? The answer is a fullness alteration that involves a series of slashes and pivots to add fabric just in the center of your pattern piece. You can use fullness alterations for adding or removing fullness at the curves on the front and back of the body, such as the bust, lower abdomen, upper back or derriere.

Once you have slashed your pattern and have the pieces positioned the way you want, tape the pieces into place. With some alterations, you may notice that the seams are a bit jagged instead of a smooth line or curve. In this case, you can either trace the pattern piece onto another piece of paper, or just tape extra paper where you need it. Use a ruler or a french curve to redraw the seams so that they're smooth. If the grainline is crooked, use a ruler to redraw that as well. To redraw a dart, simply draw lines reconnecting the endpoints with the tip.

Has your alteration affected your seams in any way? If so, find the pieces that adjoin the one you've altered and make sure they are altered as well. For example, if you've added length to the front of a skirt, add length to the back as well, so they match at the side seams.

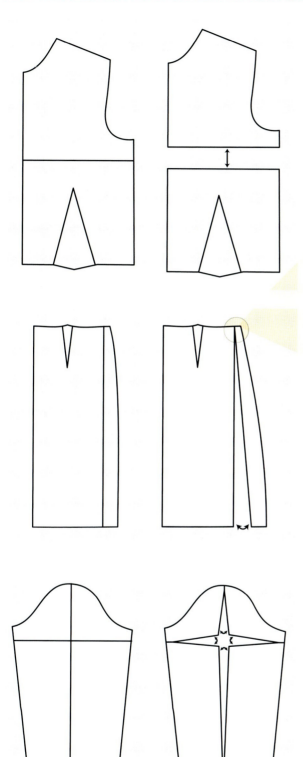

Slash Alteration
A simple slash alteration goes from one seam straight across or down, adding length and width evenly along the slash line. In this example, the slash adds length for a longer torso.

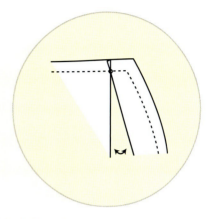

Pivot Alteration
A pivot alteration adds or removes ease along a seam, while keeping the length of other seams unchanged. Here, we're pivoting a skirt to make the hips wider.

Preserving the Seam Allowance
When you pivot along a seam, you want to make sure that you pivot on the stitching line, not in the seam allowance. Slash the line up to your pivot point and snip the seam allowance so that you can pivot without tearing the pattern.

Fullness Alteration
A fullness alteration adds or removes fullness within a pattern piece, such as at the bust, usually leaving the seams unchanged. This sample shows adding some fullness around a biceps.

HOW TO MAKE ALTERATIONS

Over the next few pages, you'll see a number of common alterations. To actually make the alterations, refer to the steps below. These steps show a pivot alteration, but are easily adapted for slash and fullness alterations.

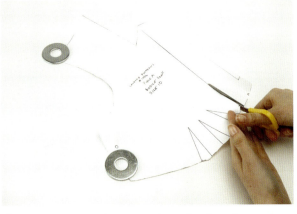

1. Transfer your pattern—the outline and all markings—to sturdier paper, such as bond paper. Mark where you plan to make the alteration. Mark the seamline on the pattern near your slash line. Measure ⅝" (1.6cm) from the edges at the top and bottom of the slash line.

2. Using paper scissors, cut along the alteration mark. For pivot alterations (and some fullness alterations), stop at the seam allowance; you'll want to keep that intact.

3. You should have determined from your muslin how much to increase/decrease the pattern. In this example, we're doing a pivot alteration and adding an inch (2.5cm) at the bottom. Add the inch (2.5cm) at the seamline, ⅝" (1.6cm) from the edge.

4. Secure with the pattern pieces in the correct position. For taping pattern pieces, I like to use blue artist's tape. It's similar to masking tape but very easy to see and made to be repositioned on paper.

SIMPLE SLASH ALTERATIONS: TORSO LENGTH

If the pattern is too short or too long for your torso, you can add or remove length to a bodice with a simple slash alteration.

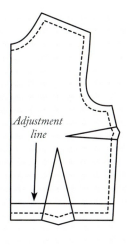
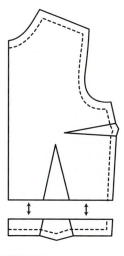
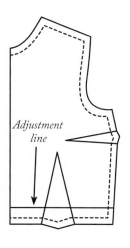
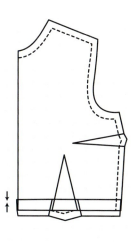

FIGURE 1A **FIGURE 2A** **FIGURE 1B** **FIGURE 2B**

LONG-WAISTED

1. Use a ruler to draw a straight line across the Bodice Front, an inch or two (2.5 cm-5.1cm) above the waistline. If the pattern provides an adjustment line, use that. (Figure 1A)

2. Spread the pattern pieces apart evenly along the slash to make the pieces longer. (Figure 2A)

3. Tape them in place. Redraw the side seams and dart.

4. Repeat the alteration on the Bodice Back.

SHORT-WAISTED

1. Use a ruler to draw a straight line across the Bodice Front, an inch or two (2.5cm-5.1cm) above the waistline. If the pattern provides an adjustment line, use that. (Figure 1B)

2. Overlap the pattern evenly along the slashes to make the pieces shorter. (Figure 2B)

3. Tape them in place. Redraw the side seams and dart.

4. Repeat the alteration on the Bodice Back.

OTHER SLASH ALTERATIONS

- *Increasing the width of a sleeve for a large arm*
- *Decreasing the width of a sleeve for a small arm*
- *Increasing the length of a skirt for someone who is tall or has long legs*
- *Decreasing the length of a skirt for someone who is short or has short legs*

PIVOT ALTERATION: SWAY BACK

With a sway back, the lower back curves inward, either from poor posture, repetitive activities or natural shape. An excess of fabric will pool in the lower back, resulting in horizontal folds of fabric. In this case, you may need to alter skirts, trousers or bodices. In the case of a dress, you'll need to alter both the bodice and skirt. When you're doing a muslin fitting for a dress, pinch out folds of fabric on both the bodice and the skirt.

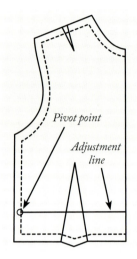 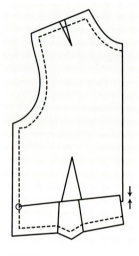 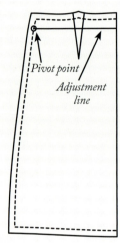 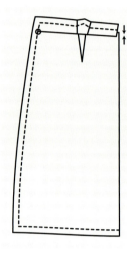

FIGURE 1A **FIGURE 2A** **FIGURE 1B** **FIGURE 2B**

BODICE

1. From your muslin, identify the point at the center back where you need to remove fabric. Mark this point on the center back.

2. Draw a line straight across to the side seam. (Figure 1A)

3. Mark the point where this line crosses the side seam. Don't include the seam allowance. This is your pivot point.

4. Slash the line up to the pivot point.

5. Pivot the pieces together and overlap to remove the desired amount of ease at the center back. (Figure 2A)

6. Tape the pieces in place. Redraw the center back and dart.

SKIRT

1. From your muslin, identify the point at the center back where you need to remove fabric. Mark this point on the center back.

2. Mark the point where the waist seam crosses the side seam. Don't include the seam allowance. This is your pivot point. (Figure 1B)

3. Draw a line straight across, as shown, and slash. Leave a hinge at the pivot point.

4. Pivot the pieces together and overlap them to remove the desired amount of ease at the center back. (Figure 2B)

5. Tape the piece in place. Redraw the center back and dart.

PIVOT ALTERATION: HIP WIDTH

If you have hips that are wider or narrower than your pattern is made for, you can do a pivot alteration to add some ease at the hips, while keeping the waist the same. You can use this technique for skirts, dresses and trousers. You will be altering both the front and back, so remember to evenly divide the total amount of width that you need to add or subtract. For example, if you need to remove 2" (5.1 cm) in circumference, divide this number by four to add ½" (1.3 cm) on each piece.

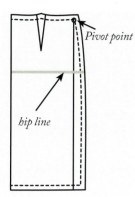
FIGURE 1A

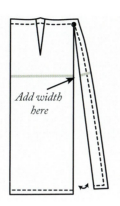
FIGURE 2A

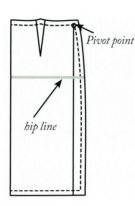
FIGURE 1B

FIGURE 2B

WIDE HIPS

1. Use a ruler to transfer the hip line that you marked on your muslin to the Skirt Front.

2. Mark the point where the side seam and waist seam meet on each. Don't include the seam allowance. This is where you will pivot.

3. Draw a line straight down from this point to the hem (Figure 1A) and slash, leaving the hinge at the top.

4. Pivot the pieces apart until you have the desired extra width at the hip line. You will have to fold that hinge a little to pivot. (Figure 2A)

5. Tape the pieces in place and redraw the hem.

6. Repeat this alteration for the Skirt Back.

NARROW HIPS

1. Use a ruler to draw the hip line on your Skirt Front.

2. Mark the point where the side seam and waist seam meet. Don't include the seam allowance. This is where you will pivot.

3. Draw a line straight down from this point to the hem (Figure 1B), and slash, leaving the hinge at the top.

4. Pivot the pieces so they overlap until you have reduced the desired width at the hip line. (Figure 2B) You may have to clip the hinge to pivot.

5. Tape the pieces in place and redraw the hem.

6. Repeat this alteration for the Skirt Back.

NO WAIST SEAM?

If you're working with a dress that doesn't have a waist seam, just cut the pieces apart at the waist and make your adjustments. Tape them back together and redraw any darts or seams

PIVOT ALTERATION: LARGE WAIST

Another common fitting problem is needing to enlarge the pattern at the waist. Again, we'll use a pivot alteration to add width at the waist. These waist alterations can be used on skirts, trousers or bodices. If you are making a dress with a waist seam, you will need to alter both the bodice and the skirt. The skirt is just slightly more complex than the bodice because you will need to make two slashes in order to keep the shape of the seams. Divide the total amount of ease you are adding by four to get the actual width you'll add to each pattern piece.

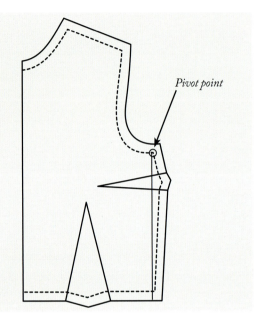

FIGURE 1A

BODICE

1. On the Bodice Front, draw your seam along the waistline. Make sure that you add the width at the stitching line, *not* the cutting line.

2. Mark the point where the side seam and underarm meet. Don't include the seam allowance. This is where you will pivot. Draw a straight line from the pivot point to the waist. (Figure 1A)

3. Slash the line up to the pivot point. Leave the hinge at the top.

4. Pivot the bodice pieces apart until you have added the desired width at the waist seam. You will have to fold in the hinge to pivot. (Figure 2A)

5. Tape the pieces in place. Redraw the waist and horizontal dart.

6. Repeat this alteration on the Bodice Back.

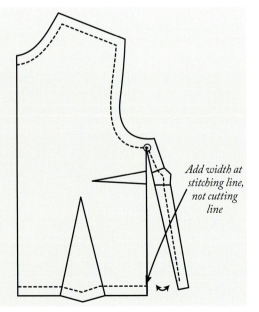

FIGURE 2A

SKIRT

1. On the Skirt Front, mark the hip line on your pattern. Mark the point where the hip line meets the side seam. Don't include the seam allowance. This is the first pivot point.

2. Draw a diagonal line to the waist, as shown in blue-green, and slash. Leave a hinge at this pivot point.

3. Mark the point on the skirt where the waist and side seams meet. Don't include the seam allowance. This is your second pivot point.

4. Draw a line from the first slash to the second pivot point, as shown in orange, and slash. Leave a hinge at this pivot point. (Figure 1B)

5. Pivot along the first slash line until you have added the desired width at the waist seam. You will have to fold in the hinge to pivot.

6. Pivot along the second slash line and overlap the pieces to straighten the waistline. You will have to slash the hinge to pivot. (Figure 2B)

7. Tape the pieces in place. Redraw the waist.

8. Repeat this alteration for the Skirt Back.

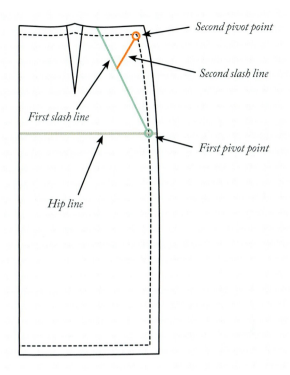

FIGURE 1B

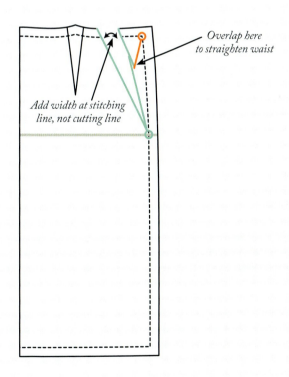

FIGURE 2B

85

PIVOT ALTERATION: SMALL WAIST

You can use a pivot alteration to remove width at the waist. These waist alterations can be used on skirts, trousers or bodices. If you're making a dress with a waist seam, you'll need to alter both the bodice and the skirt. The skirt is just slightly more complex than the bodice because you will need to make two slashes in order to keep the shape of the seams. Divide the total amount of ease you are subtracting by four to get the actual width you'll remove from each pattern piece.

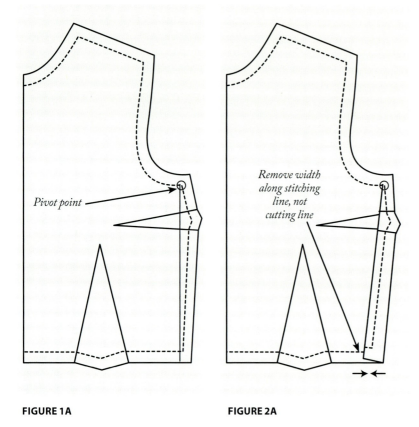

FIGURE 1A

FIGURE 2A

BODICE

1. On the Bodice Front, draw in your seams along the waistlines. You want to make sure that you remove the width at the stitching line, not the cutting line.

2. Mark the point where the side seam and underarm meet. Don't include the seam allowance. This is where you will pivot. Draw a straight line from the pivot point to the waist. (Figure 1A)

3. Slash the line up to the pivot point. Leave the hinge at the top.

4. Pivot the bodice pieces together to overlap until you have removed the desired width at the waist seam. You will have to slash the hinge to pivot. (Figure 2A)

5. Tape the pieces in place. Redraw the waist and horizontal dart.

6. Repeat this alteration on the Bodice Back.

SKIRT

1. On the Skirt Front, mark the hip line on your pattern. Mark the point where the hip line meets the side seam. Don't include the seam allowance. This is the first pivot point.

2. Draw a diagonal slash line to the waist (shown in blue-green), and slash. Leave a hinge at this pivot point.

3. Mark the point on the skirt where the waist and side seams meet. Don't include the seam allowance. This is your second pivot point.

4. Draw a diagonal line from the first slash to the second pivot point (shown in red), and slash. Leave a hinge at this pivot point. (Figure 1B)

5. Pivot along the first slash line to overlap until you have removed the desired width at the waist seam. You will have to clip the hinge to pivot.

6. Pivot along the second slash line and spread the pieces to straighten the waistline. You will have to fold the hinge to pivot. (Figure 2B)

7. Tape the pieces in place. Redraw the waist.

8. Repeat this alteration for the Skirt Back.

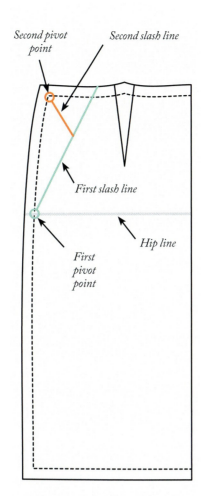

FIGURE 1B

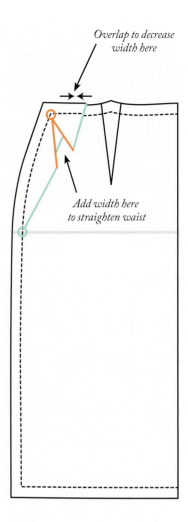

FIGURE 2B

OTHER PIVOT ALTERATIONS

- Increasing length at the upper back for round shoulders
- Increasing width at the shoulders for broad shoulders
- Decreasing width at the back for narrow shoulders

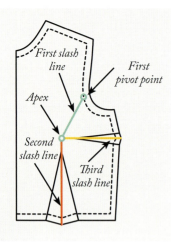

Figure 1A

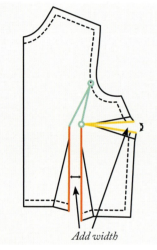

Figure 2A

Figure 3A

FULLNESS ALTERATION: BUST

Many women require alterations to accommodate a full bust. Some smaller pattern companies such as Colette Patterns draft their patterns for a C cup, which is modern average in North America, while the largest pattern companies continue to draft for a B cup. Bust size is a great example of why most patterns do not fit out of the box. There are huge numbers of women who are neither a B nor C cup, but who fall on either side. For many of us, bust adjustments will make one of the biggest possible differences in the fit of our clothing.

This is a fullness adjustment, meaning that we want to change the shape around a curve (i.e., the bust), but not necessarily the height or length of the pattern overall. This is a sort of variation on the pivot adjustment; you just need to make more slash lines to make this happen. You will also be either increasing or decreasing the width of darts in the process, which will make for a nice even curve around the bust.

LARGER BUST

1. From your muslin, identify the apex of the bust and mark that point on the Bodice Front.

2. Mark a point on the armscye seam, about halfway along the seam. Don't include the seam allowance. This is your first pivot point.

3. Draw a line from this point to the bust apex (shown in blue-green), and slash. Leave a hinge at the top.

4. Draw a line from the bust apex down through the waist dart (shown in red). Slash along this line.

5. Draw a line from the bust apex to the side seam, through the side dart (shown in yellow).

6. Slash this line almost up to the bust apex, leaving a tiny hinge. This will be the second pivot point. (Figure 1A)

7. Spread the pieces apart as shown to add the desired amount of width at the bust apex. (Figure 2A)

8. Draw a line from the bust apex to the center front and slash. (Figure 3A)

9. Move the lower center front piece down in order to bring it in line with the rest of the waistline.

10. Tape the pieces in place. Redraw the darts and seams. The tip of the dart should now be further from the apex, which leaves more room for a large bust.

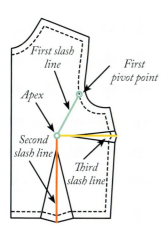

Figure 1B

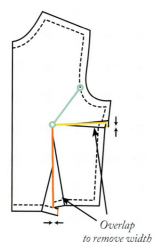

Figure 2B

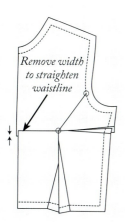

Figure 3B

SMALLER BUST

1. From your muslin, identify the apex of the bust and mark that point on the Bodice Front.

2. Mark a point on the armscye seam, about halfway along the seam. Don't include the seam allowance. This is your first pivot point.

3. Draw a line from this point to the bust apex (shown in blue-green), and slash. Leave a hinge at the top.

4. Draw a line from the bust apex down through the waist dart (shown in red). Slash along this line.

5. Draw a line from the bust apex to the side seam, through the side dart (shown in yellow).

6. Slash this line almost up to the bust apex, leaving a tiny hinge. This will be the second pivot point.

7. Overlap the pieces as shown to remove the desired amount of width at the bust apex.

8. Draw a line from the bust apex to the center front and slash.

9. Move the lower center front piece up in order to bring it in line with the rest of the waistline.

10. Tape the pieces in place. Redraw the darts and seams. The darts will now be narrower, for less room at the bust.

OTHER FULLNESS ALTERATIONS

- *Increasing fullness at the upper arm for large biceps*

- *Increasing fullness at the back of a skirt for a protruding derriere*

- *Decreasing fullness at the back of a skirt for a flat derriere*

- *Increasing fullness at the front of a skirt for a protruding lower abdomen*

Project: PASTILLE DRESS

$\mathcal{A}$ simple, well-fitted dress pattern can take you far. This cap-sleeved sheath follows the natural shape of the body for a flattering cut without much fuss. It's a dress that works in a variety of colors, fabrics and prints, and it can be easily dressed up or down with your fabric choice. The important thing with a simple dress like this is getting the right fit. With its simple adornment of three horizontal knife pleats and a small bow at the neckline, there's little decoration to interfere with getting your fit just the way you want it. Because many dresses use this kind of basic dart shaping, once you've fit a simple dress like this to your body, you'll be prepared to adjust many other patterns!

Review the fitting techniques in this chapter to determine your own fitting needs, make your pattern adjustments and then test your new fit with a muslin. With only a few pattern pieces for this dress, a muslin will be quick and easy, so you can spend the time getting the fit just the way you like it. Once you've perfected this dress for your body, it's very easy to change the details and experiment. You could get rid of the pleats, add trim or leave it completely unadorned.

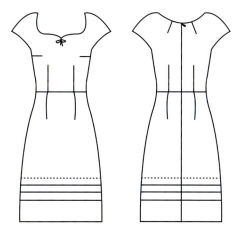

TOOLS

sewing shears (or rotary cutter and mat)

pattern weights

pins

hand sewing needle

marking pen or chalk

zipper presser foot

pinking shears (optional)

SUPPLIES

fabric (see Fabric Suggestions and Fabric Required table)

lightweight fusible interfacing (see Fabric Required table)

thread

24" (6.6cm) zipper

one small hook and eye closure

two large-holed beads

SKILLS CHECKLIST

* *Preparing your fabric (pp. 42–43)*
* *Laying out your pattern (pp. 44–45)*
* *Cutting out your pattern (pp. 50–51)*
* *Transferring the markings (pp. 48–49)*
* *Fitting a muslin (pp. 73–76)*
* *Thread tracing (p. 49)*
* *Sewing darts (pp. 20–21)*
* *Notching curves (p. 22)*
* *Sewing a centered zipper (pp. 24–25)*
* *Sewing a catchstitch by hand (p. 17)*

FABRIC SUGGESTIONS

Choose a crisp, light fabric that holds its shape well to make the most of the pleats and shaped neckline. Medium-weight fabrics, such as twill, silk dupioni, fine shirting cottons, linen or sateen, are good choices.

FABRIC REQUIRED (YARDS AND METERS):

To find your size, check the size chart at the end of the book.

	0	2	4	6	8	10	12	14	16	18
FABRIC, 45" (115 CM)	2⅔ yards (2.4 m)	2⅔ yards (2.4 m)	2¾ yards (2.5 m)	2¾ yards (2.5 m)	2¾ yards (2.5 m)	2⅞ yards (2.6 m)	2⅞ yards (2.6 m)	3 yards (2.7 m)	3 yards (2.7 m)	3 yards (2.7 m)
FABRIC, 60" (150 CM)	1¾ yards (1.6 m)	1¾ yards (1.6 m)	1¾ yards (1.6 m)	1¾ yards (1.6 m)	1¾ yards (1.6 m)	1¾ yards (1.6 m)	1⅞ yards (1.7 m)	1⅞ yards (1.7 m)	3 yards (2.7 m)	3 yards (2.7 m)
NON-WOVEN FUSIBLE INTERFACING, 20" (50 CM)	½ yard (0.5 m)	½ yard (0.5 m)	½ yard (0.5 m)	½ yard (0.5 m)	½ yard (0.5 m)	½ yard (0.5 m)	½ yard (0.5 m)	½ yard (0.5 m)	½ yard (0.5 m)	½ yard (0.5 m)

FINISHED GARMENT MEASUREMENTS (INCHES):

	0	2	4	6	8	10	12	14	16	18
BUST	33½" (85 cm)	34½" (88 cm)	35½" (90 cm)	36½" (93 cm)	38½" (98 cm)	40" (102 cm)	41½" (105 cm)	43½" (111 cm)	45½" (116 cm)	47½" (121 cm)
BACK LENGTH*	37⅝" (96 cm)	38⅛" (97 cm)	38⅝" (98 cm)	39⅛" (99 cm)	39⅝" (101 cm)	40⅛" (102 cm)	40⅝" (103 cm)	41⅛" (104 cm)	41⅝" (106 cm)	42⅛" (107 cm)
HEM WIDTH	40⅝" (103 cm)	41⅝" (106 cm)	42⅝" (108 cm)	43⅝" (111 cm)	44⅝" (113 cm)	46⅛" (117 cm)	47⅝" (120 cm)	49⅝" (126 cm)	51⅝" (131 cm)	53⅝" (136 cm)
WAIST	26" (66 cm)	27" (69 cm)	28" (71 cm)	29" (76 cm)	30" (76 cm)	31½" (77 cm)	33" (84 cm)	35" (89 cm)	37" (94 cm)	39" (99 cm)
HIP	39" (99 cm)	40" (102 cm)	41" (104 cm)	42" (107 cm)	43" (109 cm)	45½" (116 cm)	47" (119 cm)	49" (124 cm)	51" (130 cm)	53" (135 cm)

* Back length is measured from the base of your neck to the hem.

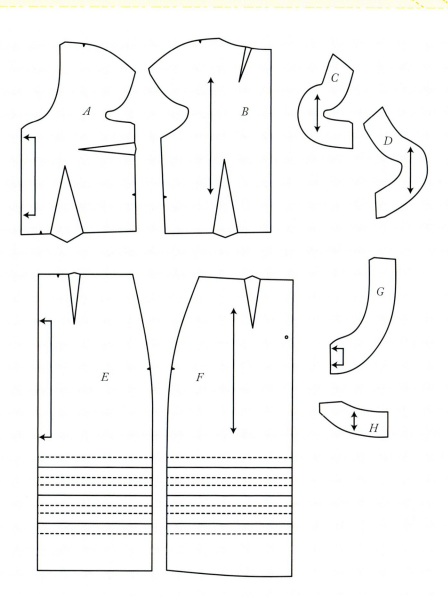

PATTERN INVENTORY

A - Bodice Front
B - Bodice Back
C - Front Sleeve Facing
D - Back Sleeve Facing
E - Skirt Front
F - Skirt Back
G - front Neck Facing
H - Back Neck Facing

All pieces include ⅝" (1.6 cm) seam allowance.

CUTTING LAYOUTS

Fabric most frequently comes in widths of 45" (115 cm) or 60" (150 cm), but widths do vary. Your cutting layout may also need to change for a napped or one-way fabric (see page 44 for details), or you may need a different layout for matching stripes or plaids (see pages 46-47).

FABRIC, 45" (115 CM):

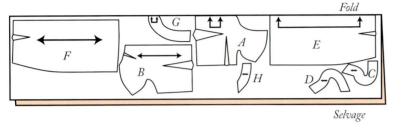

FABRIC, 60" (150 CM), SIZES 0 TO 14:

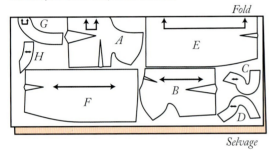

FABRIC, 60" (150 CM), SIZES 16 TO 18:

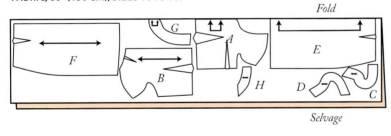

INTERFACING, 20" (50 CM):

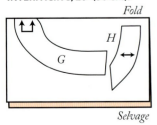

INSTRUCTIONS

MARK PLEATS

1. Transfer the pleating lines to your fabric. To do this, place the pattern on your fabric and mark the endpoints of each line. Use a ruler or straight edge to draw lines between the endpoints with chalk or a marking pen.

2. Using contrasting thread colors, baste through these lines to thread trace them, so they will be visible on both sides of your fabric. Use one color of thread for the dashed lines (the stitching lines) and another color for the solid lines (the outer fold). (Figure 1)

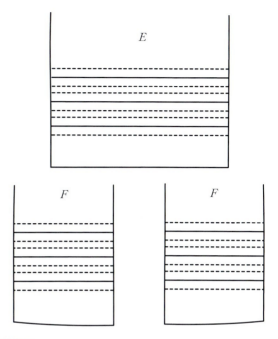

FIGURE 1

APPLY INTERFACING

1. Apply fusible interfacing to the wrong side of Front Neck Facing (G) and Back Neck Facing (H) following manufacturer's instructions for your interfacing. (Figure 2)

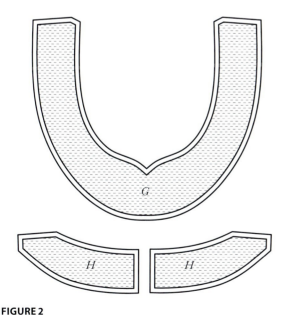

FIGURE 2

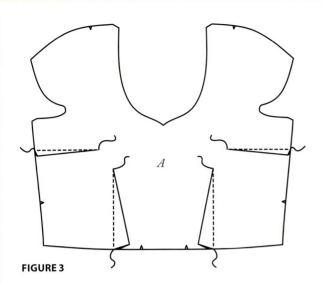

FIGURE 3

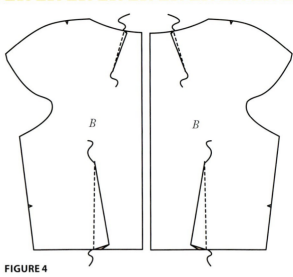

FIGURE 4

SEW FRONT DARTS

1. On Bodice Front (A), bring the legs of each dart together and pin. Stitch darts and tie off the ends.

2. Press the side darts toward the waist, and the waist darts toward the center. (Figure 3)

SEW BACK DARTS

1. On Bodice Back (B) pieces, bring the legs of each dart together and pin. Stitch darts and tie off the ends.

2. Press the darts toward the center. (Figure 4)

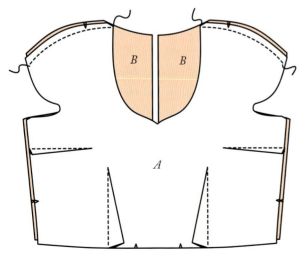

FIGURE 5

SEW SHOULDER SEAMS

1. With right sides together, stitch Bodice Front (A) to Bodice Back (B) pieces at the shoulders. Press the shoulder seams open and finish the raw edges. (Figure 5)

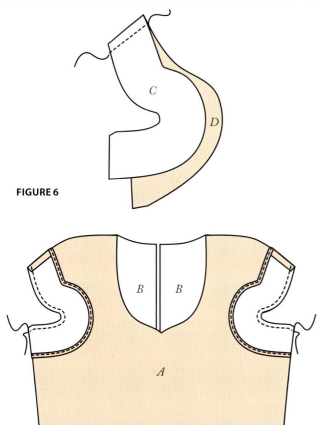

FIGURE 6

FIGURE 7

SEW SLEEVE FACING

1. With right sides together, stitch each Front Sleeve Facing (G) to a Back Sleeve Facing (H) at the shoulder. Leave it open at the underarm at this point. (Figure 4) Press the seams open and finish the raw edges of the seam.

2. Finish the outer edge of each of the two sleeve facing units by creating a narrow hem. To do this, turn the outer edge under ¼" (6 mm), notching the outer curves as necessary so that the seam will lay flat. Press the narrow hem into place and stitch.

3. With right sides together, pin the sleeve facings to the sleeve openings. Stitch into place, beginning and ending at the underarm. (Figure 7)

4. On this seam, clip the inner curves and notch the outer curves.

SEW SIDE SEAMS

1. Turn the bodice so the wrong side is facing you again, and turn the sleeve facings to the inside (right side of figure 8).

2. Baste each side together in one continuous seam, beginning at the waist and basting all the way up through the underarm of the facing. (Left side of figure 8) While basting, take care to align the underarm seams so that they meet.

3. Stitch along your basting. Remove the basting stitches.

4. Finish the raw edges. Turn the facing back to the inside and, with wrong sides of the dress and facing together (right side of figure 8), press along the armhole seam.

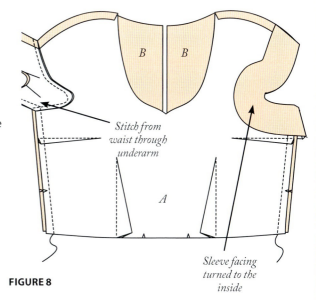

Stitch from waist through underarm

Sleeve facing turned to the inside

FIGURE 8

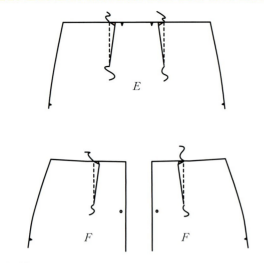

FIGURE 9

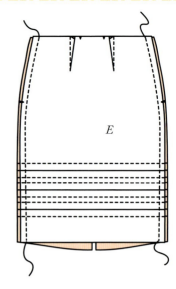

FIGURE 10

SEW SKIRT DARTS

1. On Skirt Front (C) and Skirt Back (D), bring the legs of each dart together and pin. Stitch darts and tie off the ends.

2. Press darts toward the center on both the front and back. (Figure 9)

SEW SKIRT SIDE SEAMS

1. With right sides together, stitch Skirt front (C) to Skirt Back (D) at the side seams, matching notches and pleat lines. (Figure 10) Finish the raw edges and press the seams open.

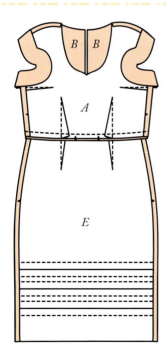

FIGURE 11

SEW BODICE TO SKIRT

1. With right sides together, pin the bodice to the skirt at the waist. Baste the waist seam, taking care to match up notches, side seams and darts.

2. Stitch the waistline. Finish the raw edges of the seam and press downward. (Figure 11)

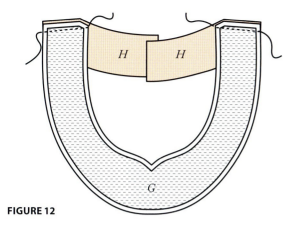

FIGURE 12

SEW NECK FACING

1. With right sides together, stitch Front Neck Facing (G) to Back Neck Facing (H) at the shoulders. (Figure 12) Press the seams open.

2. Finish the outer edge of each of the neck facing by creating a narrow hem. To do this, turn the outer edge under ¼" (6 mm), notching the outer curves as necessary so that the seam will lay flat. Press the narrow hem into place and stitch.

3. With right sides together, stitch the facing to the neck edge. (Figure 13)

4. Trim and grade the neckline seam, then notch along the seam to help reduce bulk. Be sure to cut one notch at the center front of the neckline, where it forms a point. (Figure 14) If your fabric seems to fray easily, you may wish to reinforce this center point with a second row of stitching, just inside the first.

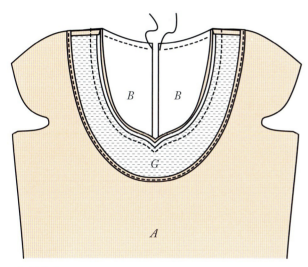

FIGURE 13

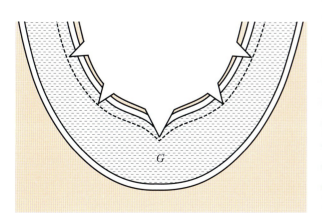

FIGURE 14

NOTCHING TIP

It can be unnerving to notch a seam close to your stitching, because there's always the danger of cutting a bit too deeply. To prevent this, you can place a pin through your fabric at the point you want to cut to. The pin should be just inside of the stitching line and parallel to it. The pin will prevent the tip of your shears from cutting too deeply.

INSERT ZIPPER

1. With right sides together, stitch the Skirt Back (F) pieces together at the center back, leaving open above the large circle.

2. Using a zipper foot on your sewing machine, sew the zipper into the center back seam above the large circle. I recommend sewing a centered zipper. For detailed instructions on this technique, see the section on zippers in chapter six.

3. Turn the back edges of the facing under and press. Hand stitch the facing to the zipper tape using a catchstitch. (Figure 15)

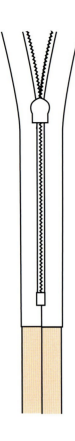

FIGURE 15

PLEAT SKIRT

1. On the skirt, bring the stitching lines of each pleat together, folding along the outer fold line between them, and pin.

2. Stitch the three pleats, remove thread tracing and press downward. (Figure 16)

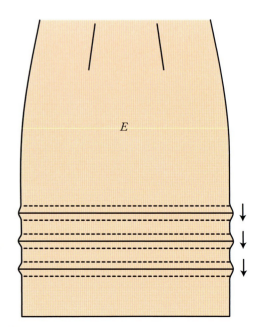

FIGURE 16

FIGURE 17

CREATE BOW

1. To create the bow, cut a strip of your fabric 1" (2.5 cm) wide and 16" (40.6 cm) long. Fold the strip in half lengthwise and, with right sides together, stitch down the length, using a ¼" (6mm) seam allowance. Trim the seam to ⅛" (3mm). (Figure 17)

2. Turn the tube right side out using a loop turner. If you don't have a loop turner, you can also use a safety pin. Attach the safety pin to one end of the tube, then pass it through the tube to the other side and pull gently.

3. Thread two large beads onto the ends of the tube, and tie each end in a single knot. Tie the tube into a bow, and secure the bow to the center front neckline with a few stitches.

FINISHING

1. Form a turned hem on the skirt. Turn the hem under ¼" (6mm) and press. Turn again ⅜" (1 cm), press and stitch into place.

2. To secure facings in place, tack them at the shoulder seams with a few stitches. Tack the sleeve facing to the inside at the side seam.

EMBELLISHMENT IDEAS

Once I have the fit down on a dress, I love to make it again and again in different fabrics. It's like a little shortcut to a great dress. Besides trying out different fabrics, there are countless embellishments you can add. Try some of these out when you're dreaming up alternate versions of your favorite patterns:

* *Add piping or another narrow trim to your seams.*
* *Topstitch your seams and edges in a contrasting thread.*
* *Substitute bias binding for facings on cuffs and necklines (see pages 136–137).*
* *Add fun buttons or simple beading.*
* *Instead of one fabric, use two colors or patterns for a two-tone effect.*
* *Sew on vintage appliqués. Lace ones are particularly pretty.*
* *Add patch pockets made from simple squares of fabric, with the edges turned under.*
* *Learn a few embroidery stitches and add embroidered flowers.*
* *Make matching accessories, like a covered belt or scarf.*

Chapter Five: A BEAUTIFUL FABRIC

*T*extiles are one of the most inspiring artistic materials you could dream of. They are created from a wide variety of raw materials, from the cocoons of silk worms to the stalks of bamboo, each with its own particular merits. These fibers are formed into cloth based on traditional techniques from around the world, producing fabrics in a stunning array of textures, weights and densities. And perhaps most energizing of all, these textiles can be dyed vibrant or subtle colors, or printed with gorgeous patterns. With all of this sumptuous variety at your fingertips, learning a bit about fabric can truly elevate your sewing by giving you a deeper understanding of the materials you are primarily working with.

There are two ways to know your fabric. First, there is the sensory understanding, the seemingly natural way we respond to a fabric's texture, color and feel. Personal taste is a large part of this understanding, but it's also a matter of training your eye. The more you work with fabric, the better your intuitions about a fabric's hand and drape, and the better you become at visualizing the fabric as a completed garment. Experience is the best teacher for tuning into how fabrics work.

The second way is a technical understanding. There is a huge variety of textiles in the world, and being able to interpret the language around fabric will greatly enhance your ability to work with them. The technical understanding serves to strengthen the sensory understanding by giving voice to all the many qualities of cloth, allowing you a stronger understanding of how to use them.

Think of it this way: Having a sensory understanding of fabric is like being a good storyteller, and having the technical understanding is like knowing how to read and write. Of course you can be a great storyteller without knowing how to read, but gaining that knowledge allows you to expand your vocabulary, discover new ways to express yourself and share your ideas more easily.

CHOOSING FABRIC

Fabric is your most important raw material in sewing, and the characteristics of the fabric you choose will have a dramatic effect on your project. Choosing a beautiful fabric that you love and that fits your project both aesthetically and technically is probably the most fascinating creative challenge in sewing.

Impulsive fabric choices are a common sewing pitfall. It's so easy to become overwhelmed with choices at the fabric store, that you just pick up anything that has a pretty color or cute pattern. This can lead to a mix-and-match approach, where fabric and design are paired without much attention to the qualities of each. Sometimes this works and sometimes it doesn't.

My approach is a little different. I find that garments usually start in one of two ways. In the first case, I have a design in mind and need to find the right fabric for it. In this case, I note the qualities of the fabric that I am looking for, then set about looking for fabrics within those parameters. It's a bit like a treasure hunt. In the second case, I'm inspired by a fabric first, and use that as my starting point. With this reverse approach, I think about which designs would work best with the qualities of the fabric. As you can see, in both cases, the fundamental qualities of the fabric are essential to putting the whole garment together.

There is a lot of vocabulary built around textiles. Becoming familiar with the language of fabric will help you understand which materials you respond to and why, and over time it will inform nearly every aspect of your sewing. But let's start with the most apparent aspects of fabric, the qualities you notice when you first pick up a fabric at the store.

FABRIC QUALITIES

There's a lot you can learn about textiles, but the sensory qualities of the fabric, which you can easily recognize when you're looking through the bolts at your local store, are both the easiest to gauge and the most important to your sewing. These are the aspects of the fabric that you can see with your eyes or feel with your hands. Here are some of the qualities to think about:

104

STRETCH

Stretch can come from knit fabrics, or fabrics that incorporate elastic. Knits require special techniques for sewing. Nonstretch fabrics are the most common and are suitable for the majority of projects.

Nonstretchy:
Light Rayon Twill

Stretchy:
Silk Jersey

TEXTURE

Texture on fabric can be bold or subtle, from a crinkle to a thick nubby weave to a subtle brushed softness. Smooth, less textured fabrics are easy to incorporate in your sewing, putting the focus more on the color or print.

Textured:
Crinkled Silk Chiffon

Smooth:
Silk Crepe de Chine

SHEEN

Shiny fabrics reflect light and can be beautiful and eye-catching. They also draw attention to curves, lumps and wrinkles. Fabrics can have a great deal of shine, or a more subtle lustre. Matte fabrics absorb light rather than reflect it, resulting in a dull finish that smooths out lumps and bumps in a flattering way.

Shiny:
Silk Charmeuse

Matte:
Silk Crepe

WEIGHT

Heavy fabrics are just that: They are thicker and have greater weight. With heavy fabrics, it's important to think about whether the fabric will add too much bulk, especially if your design is fitted. Light fabrics are thin and feel less weighty in your hand. They may even be sheer.

Heavy:
Melton Wool

Light:
Silk Chiffon

Stiffer: Silk Twill

Drapey: Silk Crepe

DRAPE

Stiffer fabrics have what is called "body." They are crisp and tend to stand away from the body more easily, making them a great choice for structured, fitted garments. Drapey fabrics have more fluidity and hang beautifully. See the sidebar to learn more about both body and drape.

DRAPE AND BODY

The qualities of drape and body are perhaps the most overlooked in home sewing, but have a profound impact on the look of your clothing. A fabric with body is stiff, and so it can be sculpted around the body with seams and darts, making it ideal for structured garments like jackets. Fabrics with drape are fluid, falling gracefully and clinging easily to the body, making it perfect for flowing garments.

It's easy to confuse these qualities with weight, mistakenly believing that heavy fabrics are, by their nature, stiff and light fabrics are always drapey. While this is often true, the two don't match up exactly. There are heavier fabrics that flow, such as a heavy wool crepe, and light fabrics that are stiff, such as organza. And fabrics of the same weight can have dramatic differences in their drape.

When you're hunting for fabric, be sure to consider the amount of drape you'd like. Try unrolling a little from the bolt and draping it over some neighboring bolts to see how it falls. Grasp the fabric by the corner and hold it up, taking a look at the way it drapes along the bias, like in the photo. Drapey fabrics have less integrity and will collapse downward, like the silk crepe below on the left. Fabrics with body will maintain their shape more when held along the bias, like the silk twill below on the right. Visualize these characteristics in the garment you're planning to make.

FABRIC BASICS

There are many ways to describe a fabric. You can talk about its sensory qualities, such as weight and drape, or you can describe it in terms of how it's made. Each piece of fabric is made of small threads that are created from a wide variety of plant, animal or chemical sources. Those threads are then joined together, either by weaving or knitting, to form a piece of fabric. So when you describe a textile, you can talk about its fiber content (wool, silk, polyester), how it's made (woven, knit) or the type of weave it has (twill, satin).

FIBERS

To create fabric, first some sort of fiber is spun into threads. These fibers can be natural, from plant or animal sources, or they can be synthetic. In addition to these natural fibers, there are a variety of synthetic fibers used in textiles, including nylon and polyester. While fabrics like polyester have positive aspects, such as their ability to withstand wrinkles, this comes with some costs. Polyester is not breathable and is difficult to press while sewing. It's best in very small doses when blended with other fabrics like cotton, but I generally advise you to stick to the naturals when you can.

Silk

Silk is a fiber that comes from the cocoons of silkworms, and its structure gives it a lustrous quality. It is wonderfully comfortable to wear, keeping you warm in the winter but cool in summer. It also takes dye well, which is why you can find it in such beautifully saturated colors.

Wool

Wool is made from the sheared hair of animals, usually sheep. It is warm but breathable, and some varieties, such as cashmere, are extremely soft while others can be coarse or itchy.

Rayon

Rayon is produced from cellulose, and while it is neither entirely natural nor entirely synthetic, it does behave very much like a natural fiber. It often appears as a lustrous fabric similar to silk. It is wonderful for keeping cool in hot weather.

Cotton

Cotton is a versatile fiber made from the cotton plant, and has become the dominant fiber used in clothing today. Cotton fabrics are comfortable and soft, and come in a variety of qualities and prices.

Linen

Linen fibers come from the flax plant, and are extremely strong, durable and soft. Lining is cool and breathable, but linen fabrics do tend to wrinkle easily.

WARP, WEFT AND GRAIN

Once fibers are made into threads, the threads must be combined together to form a fabric, and this is most often done by weaving them together. Woven fabrics are the most versatile and varied, and they are probably the fabrics you will sew most. Wovens are created on a loom. Long threads are stretched taut on the loom lengthwise, and another set of threads is passed under and over these threads crosswise to form a cloth. The lengthwise threads are called the warp, and the crosswise threads that are woven through are called the weft. The edges that are created along the length of the fabric are called the selvage. You can see the selvage clearly on almost any piece of fabric you buy. These edges look slightly different from the rest of the fabric, and they don't fray.

The grain refers to the direction the threads run in the fabric. There is a lengthwise grain, which runs parallel to the selvage a long the warp threads. You usually lay your pattern pieces along the lengthwise grain. The crosswise grain runs across the fabric, from selvage to selvage, along the warp threads. When you cut or tear your fabric off the bolt, you do so along the crosswise grain.

Last, you have the bias grain, which is diagonal. The true bias runs at 45 degrees to the other grains. Woven fabrics stretch along the bias, so that cutting your pattern pieces along the bias allows you to create a flowing, stretchy, but less stable garment. Sewing pieces cut on the bias can produce magnificent results, but often requires special techniques.

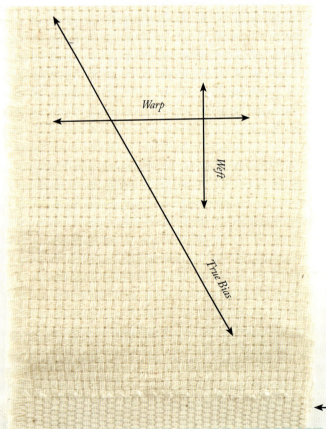

110

WEAVES

The warp and weft fibers can be woven together in a number of different ways to create various textures and effects. It's helpful to know some of these weaves in order to understand fabric terms. When you hear that a fabric is satin for example, you will know that that refers to how the fabric is made, rather than what the fabric is made from. There are three main types of weaves while others—such as pique, oxford and jacquard—are derived from these.

Plain Weave
A plain weave is a simple and sturdy weave, in which the threads form a crisscross pattern. Many fabrics have a plain weave, including taffeta, cotton lawn, organza and many others.

Twill
A twill fabric is woven with a diagonal ribbing pattern, and each side of the fabric looks different, so that it has a right and wrong side. Denim, gabardine and herringbone all have a twill weave.

Satin
Satin fabrics are woven to produce a sheen. Examples of satin fabrics are silk charmeuse, duchess satin or cotton sateen.

KNITS

Knits are created in a completely different way from wovens. Knit fabrics are made on knitting machines that create tiny loops of thread, just like you'd see in a hand knit sweater made on good old fashioned knitting needles. The main difference is the machines can handle much smaller thread to produce fine, or tightly knitted, fabrics.

Knit
Knit fabric has a great deal of stretch, making knits comfortable and easy to fit. On the other hand, all that stretch means you should use a few special techniques to handle knits, such as a ball-point needle to avoid tearing the fabric's threads, and stitches that will accommodate stretch, such as zigzag or serging. You should also use patterns specifically designed for knits. Because knits do not have the range of qualities that woven fabrics do, we'll focus mostly on wovens. Check out the Suggested Reading section (pages 156-157) if you're interested in learning more on working with knits.

COMMON FABRICS

So far, we've talked about the sensory qualities of fabrics, what they're made from and how they're made. But in addition to all of these properties, many fabrics also have specific names to help you identify them. Even experienced sewists can face confusion over all of these names, given the huge variety of garment textiles in existence. I like to keep fabric swatches on hand, which I simply pin together with a safety pin. I label each one with its name and fiber on a piece of masking tape. This is a great brainstorming tool when you're planning which type of fabric to look for, since you can feel each fabric in your hand. It also helps you become familiar with fabric names over time. These are a few of the more common fabric names you might encounter.

Chiffon
A very light, transparent fabric that drapes beautifully, especially when made from silk. Chiffon is very delicate.
Fibers used: silk, rayon or polyester.

Organza
Light, sheer and stiff fabric that looks beautiful on its own, or can be used as nonbulky interfacing or interlining for other light fabrics.
Fibers used: silk, rayon or polyester.

Batiste
A sheer and very light cotton fabric, batiste is a breathable summery fabric. It's often used with lace in heirloom sewing. Voile is very similar to batiste.
Fibers used: cotton.

Habotai (China silk)
A lightweight silk often used as a lining fabric. It's a bit light for garments, but makes a comfortable lining.
Fibers used: silk.

Georgette
Georgette is semisheer, but not as light as chiffon. It's available in a variety of prints.
Fibers used: silk or polyester.

Lawn
Lawn is a light combed cotton with a nice balance of crispness and drape. Fine lawns have a very soft, almost silky surface texture.
Fibers used: cotton.

Shirting
Cotton fabric specifically suited for tailored shirts and available in a wide range of qualities. Quality shirtings hold a crease beautifully. Think of men's dress shirts.
Fibers used: cotton.

Crepe
Crepe has a very slightly crinkled texture and beautiful drape. It is available in a range of thicknesses.
Fibers used: silk, polyester, rayon, or wool.

Charmeuse
A satin weave fabric, which is shiny on one side and a crepe texture on the other, charmeuse flows beautifully over the body.
Fibers used: silk, rayon or polyester.

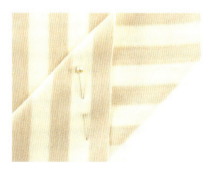

Jersey
A common knit fabric with a casual appearance and good stretch.
Fibers used: cotton, wool, silk, rayon, nylon or polyester blends.

QUILTING COTTONS

At most fabric stores, you will probably find a large variety of cottons in fun prints made especially for quilting. Often referred to as quilting cottons, these adorable and plentiful fabrics are what many new sewists turn to for making garments. Unfortunately, these short-staple cottons do not drape very well, making them unsuitable for many types of clothing. They can still work for simple garments, such as skirts, where stiffness isn't a problem, but be aware that they won't get much softer over time. Fabrics made specifically for garments will often produce nicer results.

Flannel
A brushed fabric with a soft texture. Cotton flannel is used in lighter garments like shirts, and wool flannel in heavier garments like suits and jackets, though wool flannel can also be used for heavy shirts.
Fibers used: cotton or wool.

Gabardine
A wonderful fabric, usually wool, with a tight twill weave. Wool gabardine is a great choice for tailored garments, as it's quite resistant to wrinkling.
Fibers used: wool, silk, rayon.

Tweed
A sturdy wool fabric, with a great deal of texture and multiple colors woven through for a flecked or mottled appearance.
Fibers used: wool.

Dupioni
Dupioni is a stiff fabric woven from irregular threads, creating slubs in the fabric. It is crisp and luminous, but frays easily.
Fibers used: silk.

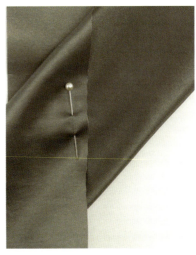

Taffeta
A very crisp fabric, most often seen in party or wedding dresses.
Fibers used: silk, rayon, polyester or nylon.

Worsted Wool
A sturdy wool suiting fabric, which also makes great skirts.
Fibers used: wool.

INTERFACING

Interfacing is a special fabric that's attached to facings to add stability, strength or crispness. There are three primary types of interfacing: woven, nonwoven or knit, and each has its own characteristics. They can either be fused to the fabric with your iron (called fusible interfacing) or sewn to the facing (called sew-in interfacing). The number of commercial interfacings available can be overwhelming, since each will produce slightly different results. But there's no need to feel overwhelmed. As with many of the learning curves in sewing, it's a matter of just a little knowledge and a lot of experimentation.

The most important thing to remember is that the interfacing should not substantially alter the qualities of the fabric. If your fabric is light and drapey, look for a light interfacing. Hold the interfacing and fabric together and drape it over your hand to examine the qualities. Test interfacings with swatches of fabric before you sew. And when you sew a garment, notice how the interfacing affects the fabric.

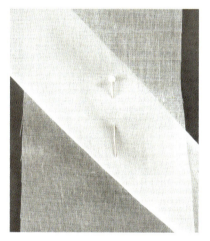

Woven Interfacings
Woven interfacings offer strength and are available in breathable natural fibers. You aren't just limited to commercial offerings, but can use many different fashion fabrics as a woven interfacing, such as cotton lawn, muslin or batiste. Silk organza makes the perfect interfacing for light silks because it adds crispness, but doesn't add bulk. You have almost limitless choice for using fabrics as a woven interfacing!

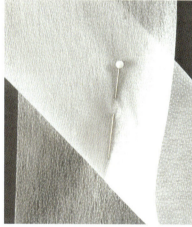

Nonwoven Interfacings
Nonwoven interfacings are made from webs of fibers that are bonded together. They may or may not have stretch and provide very nice results without adding a lot of bulk.

Knit Interfacings
Knit interfacings are generally softer and more drapey than the others and allow stretch, which is helpful if the facing needs to curve around a body. They are not as stable as wovens or nonwovens.

THREAD

After you've selected your fabric, you need to consider what thread and needle will work best with it.

THREAD

Choosing thread can be a complicated business. You want a thread that will be fine enough to glide easily through the fabric and be nearly invisible, but you don't want it to be so fine that it might break. If a thread is too thick, it can snag and pucker your fabric, and if it's too strong, it can actually cause a delicate fabric to tear. If you're experiencing any of these problems, try switching to a different sort of thread and you may find your problems disappear like magic.

Polyester thread is your basic, "all-purpose" thread, and it is suitable for most fabrics. It's a strong, elastic thread and will be your choice for the majority of projects. Go for a higher quality thread over the bargain spools and save yourself some tears.

Cotton thread is smooth and flexible, but it has no elasticity at all, so it's unsuitable for any fabric with stretch. It works well for medium- or lightweight cotton fabrics, such as lawns and shirtings.

Silk thread is very strong, and so it is not recommended for fine fabrics where it can actually tear the fabric at the seams. But it is ideal for basting, because it is almost invisible when pressed. It's also used in tailoring because it holds its shape well.

Topstitching thread or buttonhole twist is a heavier, decorative thread.

cotton thread

polyester thread

silk thread

topstitching thread

NEEDLES

Always use a needle that's appropriate to your fabric. Because the needle creates tiny holes in your fabric, a needle that's too large can create perforations that weaken your seams, while a needle that's too small can cause your thread to break. If you're facing problems while sewing, make sure you have the correct needle. Use this chart to guide you.

FABRIC WEIGHT	EXAMPLES	NEEDLE SIZE
Very light	chiffon, organza	65/9 or 70/10
Light	voile, lawn, silk crepe, charmeuse	80/12
Medium	linen, shirting, wool crepe, poplin	90/14
Semi-heavy	gabardine, tweed, coating fabrics	100/16
Heavy	canvas, denim, ticking	110/18
Knits	jersey, doubleknit, tricot	80/12 ballpoint needle

70/10 with organza

80/12 with lawn

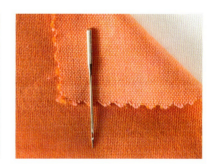
90/14 with shirting

100/16 with coating

110/18 with denim

80/12 ballpoint with jersey

PRINTS AND PATTERN

Few things are as inspiring as a beautiful patterned fabric. Patterns in fabric can either be printed onto the fabric, or actually woven in when the fabric is made. You can usually tell when a pattern is woven because it carries through to the wrong side as well, whereas a print will almost always look different on each side.

It takes some practice and experimentation to pair prints with the right clothing design. Scale is a big factor, with large prints producing a bold look that can sometimes be hard to balance with other clothing.

Some patterns are directional, meaning they look different if held upside down. The novelty print here, for example, wouldn't make sense the other way because the ladies pictured would be upside down. In this case, you'll need to use a one-way layout when cutting fabric. See pages 44-47 for more on working with directional prints like this.

Stripes

Plaid

Dots

Floral

Geometric

Paisley

Abstract

Novelty print/Conversation print

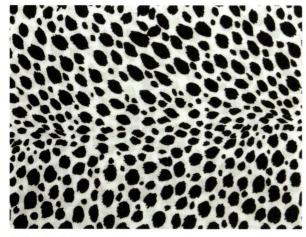
Animal print

Toile

TRICKY FABRICS

Some fabrics need a bit of special handling. These notorious fabrics are famous for causing sewing headaches, but learning just a few simples rules will have you bending them to your will.

FAUX FUR

Faux fur can be great for adding details like a furry collar of cuffs. When laying out the pattern pieces, be sure that they face the same direction (a one-way layout), so that the fur lays correctly in the final garment. Keep in mind that the nap of the fur runs down.

Cutting the Faux Fur Fabric
Transfer the pattern onto the wrong side of the faux fur. Cut your pieces with just the tip of your scissors, trying to cut through only the backing and leaving the fur intact.

Preparing to Sew Faux Fur
Comb the fur away from the seams before sewing.

Finishing
After sewing, use the comb to pick out some of the fur caught in the seam.

SLIPPERY FABRICS

For light or slippery fabrics that slide right off your cutting table, stabilize the fabric before cutting and sewing—it helps immensely. Spray stabilizers make this easy, and simply wash out when the garment is done. Be sure to prewash any fabric before using a spray stabilizer.

DENIM

The main thing that makes denim tricky is its thickness. Bulky seams can be hard to sew through, especially when several seams meet up. But the thickness and denseness of this twill cotton fabric is also its greatest asset, making clothing that is durable, strong and ages well. Imagine adding your own unique details to even your most humble and utilitarian clothing.

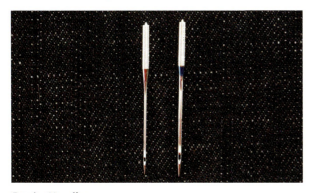

Denim Needles
Use a denim needle for this very heavy fabric. Denim needles are very strong, so there's less chance of your needle breaking as it tackles heavy fabrics. They also have a sharp point, which helps prevent skipped stitches.

A Sewing Hammer
Sewing through thick denim seams can be tough and may result in skipped stitches. To solve this problem, and also reduce bulkiness, use a sewing hammer to whack thick seams. A sewing hammer will help you compress bulky seams in any type of heavy fabric.

VELVET AND CORDUROY

Velvet and corduroy both have pile, short fibers that stick out from the fabric giving it that signature softness. Silk and rayon velvets are particularly soft and lustrous, while cotton corduroys are durable and can have beautiful color and depth for everyday wear. There are two main challenges to sewing with velvet and corduroy. First, you must make sure the nap faces the same direction on all of your pieces, and second you should take care not to crush the pile.

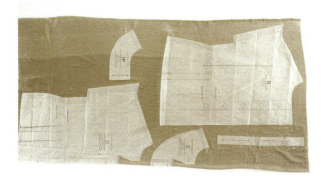

Laying on the Pattern Pieces
These fabrics have a distinct nap, and so all pieces should be cut with the tops facing the same direction (called a one-way layout).

Pressing the Fabric
It's best to avoid pressing corduroy or velvet in order to prevent crushing the pile, but if you must—like when you need to press a seam—lay a piece of matching fabric on your ironing board right-side up. Laying the right sides together this way helps preserve the pile of the fabric.

Project

TRUFFLE DRESS

Do you love dresses that are crisp and tailored? Or do you prefer something with a bit of flowing movement? This dress can give you the best of both worlds; its style rests largely on the fabric choices you make. While the bodice is lined in a crisp fabric that gives the upper portion structure, the skirt can be made sharp and stiff or soft and flowing. It's up to you. You could make a fancy version in shining silk dupioni for a special occasion, or a dressed-down modern version in light flowing cotton. It would look equally lovely in a solid or print. The fabric you choose is what really makes this dress.

With a simple wide scoop neck and darts, the shape of the bodice is simple and flattering. The straight skirt has an asymmetrical flounce trailing diagonally across the front, creating a look that could be either fancy or sleek. Experiment by examining the qualities of various fabrics, looking at their weight, drape and texture. Imagine color and print possibilities when you're choosing your materials. This dress makes a perfect canvas for playing with fabric.

TOOLS

sewing shears (or rotary cutter and mat)
pattern weights
pins
hand sewing needle
marking pen or chalk
invisible zipper presser foot
pinking shears (optional)

SUPPLIES

shell fabric (see Fabric Suggestions and Fabric Required table)
bodice lining fabric (see Fabric Suggestions and Fabric Required table)
thread
24" (61cm) invisible zipper
one small hook and eye closure

SKILLS CHECKLIST

* *Preparing your fabric (pp. 42–43)*
* *Laying out your pattern (pp. 44–45)*
* *Cutting out your pattern (pp. 50–51)*
* *Transferring the markings (pp. 48–49)*
* *Fitting a muslin (pp. 73–76)*
* *Choosing a fabric (pp. 104–107)*
* *Sewing darts (pp. 20–21)*
* *Notching curves (p. 22)*
* *Sewing an invisible zipper (p. 23)*

FABRIC SUGGESTIONS

This is a chance for you to think strategically about fabric. This dress can work in either a stiff fabric with a lot of body or a flowing, drapey fabric. Because the bodice of the dress is lined, the trick is choosing the right combination of fabrics.

The bodice of this dress is simple and tailored, so it needs a little structure. Choose a lining fabric with body, such as a light dupioni, silk twill or a crisp cotton batiste. This will help shape the bodice by providing structure and stiffness.

For the outer shell fabric, think about the effect you want it to achieve. For a flowing look, choose a drapey fabric such as silk crepe, cotton lawn, rayon challis or wool crepe. On the other hand, if you want to go for a more architectural style, use a crisp fabric such as batiste, dupioni, taffeta or cotton sateen.

Hold a swatch of the lining fabric along with a swatch of the shell fabric, and examine them in your hand. See how they feel both separately and together. Drape a bit of fabric and see how it will look as it cascades across the skirt.

FABRIC REQUIRED (YARDS AND METERS):

	0	2	4	6	8	10	12	14	16	18
SHELL FABRIC, 45" (115 CM)	3 yards (2.7 m)	3 yards (2.7 m)	3⅛ yards (2.9 m)	3⅛ yards (2.9 m)	3⅛ yards (2.9 m)	3¼ yards (3 m)	3¼ yards (3 m)	3¼ yards (3 m)	3½ yards (3.2 m)	3½ yards (3.2 m)
SHELL FABRIC, 60" (150 CM)	2⅝ yards (2.4 m)	2⅝ yards (2.4 m)	2⅝ yards (2.4 m)	2⅝ yards (2.4 m)	2¾ yards (2.5 m)	2¾ yards (2.5 m)	2¾ yards (2.5 m)	2⅞ yards (2.6 m)	2⅞ yards (2.6 m)	2⅞ yards (2.6 m)
LINING FABRIC, 45" (115 CM)	1 yard (0.9 m)	1 yard (0.9 m)	1 yard (0.9 m)	1 yard (0.9 m)	1 yard (0.9 m)	1 yard (0.9 m)	1 yard (0.9 m)	1 yard (0.9 m)	1 yard (0.9 m)	1 yard (0.9 m)
LINING FABRIC, 60" (150 CM)	⅔ yard (0.6 m)	⅔ yard (0.6 m)	⅔ yard (0.6 m)	⅔ yard (0.6 m)	⅔ yard (0.6 m)	⅔ yard (0.6 m)	⅔ yard (0.6 m)	⅔ yard (0.6 m)	⅔ yard (0.6 m)	⅔ yard (0.6 m)

FINISHED GARMENT MEASUREMENTS (INCHES):

To find your size, check the size chart at the end of the book.

	0	2	4	6	8	10	12	14	16	18
BUST	34" (86 cm)	35" (89 cm)	36" (91 cm)	37" (94 cm)	38" (97 cm)	39½" (100 cm)	41" (104 cm)	43" (109 cm)	45" (114 cm)	47" (119 cm)
BACK LENGTH*	36" (91 cm)	36½" (93 cm)	37" (94 cm)	37½" (99 cm)	38" (97 cm)	38½" (98 cm)	39" (99 cm)	39½" (100 cm)	40" (102 cm)	40½" (103 cm)
HEM WIDTH	45" (114 cm)	46" (117 cm)	47" (119 cm)	48" (122 cm)	49" (124 cm)	50½" (128 cm)	52" (132 cm)	55" (140 cm)	57" (145 cm)	59" (150 cm)
WAIST	26" (66 cm)	27" (69 cm)	28" (71 cm)	29" (74 cm)	30" (76 cm)	31½" (80 cm)	33" (84 cm)	35" (89 cm)	37" (94 cm)	39" (99 cm)
HIP	38½" (98 cm)	39½" (100 cm)	40½" (103 cm)	41½" (105 cm)	42½" (108 cm)	44" (112 cm)	45½" (116 cm)	47½" (121 cm)	49½" (126 cm)	51½" (131 cm)

* Back length is measured from the base of your neck to the hem.

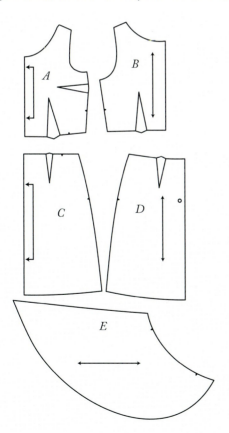

PATTERN INVENTORY

A - Bodice Front
B - Bodice Back
C - Skirt Front
D - Skirt Back
E - Skirt Drape

All pieces include ⅝" (1.6 cm) seam allowance.

CUTTING LAYOUTS

Fabric most frequently comes in widths of 45" (115 cm) or 60" (150 cm), but widths do vary. Your cutting layout may also need to change for a napped or one-way fabric (see page 44 for details), or you may need a different layout for matching stripes or plaids (see pages 46-47).

SHELL FABRIC, 45" (115 CM):

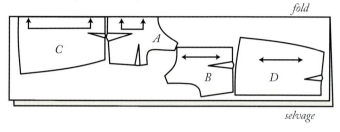

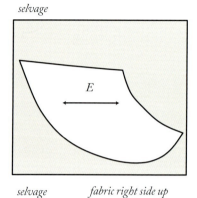

LINING FABRIC, 45" (115 CM):

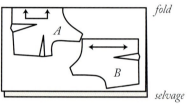

SHELL FABRIC, 60" (150 CM):

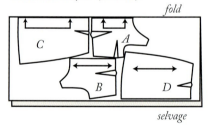

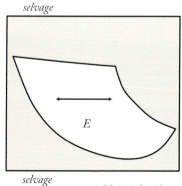

LINING FABRIC, 60" (150 CM):

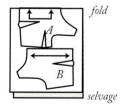

INSTRUCTIONS

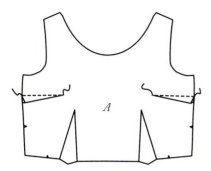

FIGURE 1

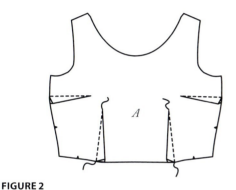

FIGURE 2

SEW BODICE FRONT DARTS

1. On Bodice Front (A), bring the legs of the horizontal side bust darts together and pin. Stitch darts and tie off ends.

2. Press the darts down, toward the waist. (Figure 1)

3. Repeat to sew the side bust darts on the Bodice Front (A) lining piece.

4. On Bodice Front (A), bring the legs of the waist darts together and pin. Stitch darts and tie off ends.

5. Press darts toward center. (Figure 2)

6. Repeat to sew the waist darts on the Bodice Front (A) lining piece.

SEW BODICE BACK DARTS

1. On each Bodice Back (B) piece, bring the legs of the waist darts together and pin. Stitch darts and tie off ends.

2. Press darts toward center back edges. (Figure 3)

3. Repeat to sew the waist darts on the Bodice Back (B) lining pieces.

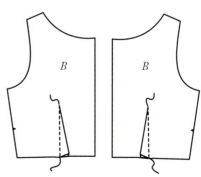

FIGURE 3

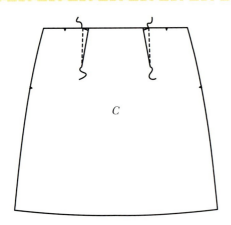

FIGURE 4

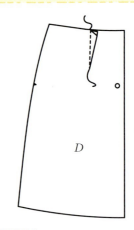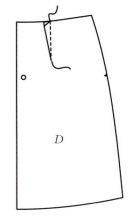

FIGURE 5

SEW SKIRT FRONT DARTS

1. On Skirt Front (C), bring the legs of the waist darts together and pin. Stitch darts and tie off ends.

2. Press darts toward center. (Figure 4)

SEW SKIRT BACK DARTS

1. On each Skirt Back (D) piece, bring the legs of the waist darts together and pin. Stitch darts and tie off ends.

2. Press darts toward center back edges. (Figure 5)

CURVED HEMS

Before turning and pressing your hem, sew a line of machine-basting. For this drape, you would baste ¼" (6mm) from the edge. Notch along the edge at even intervals, but don't cut through the basting stitches. Then turn your hem along the basting stitches and press. The stitches act as a sort of perforation, making it much easier to turn the hem evenly. Turn again, press, and stitch to complete the narrow hem.

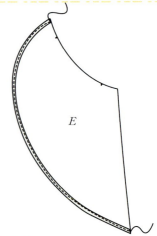

FIGURE 6

SEW DRAPE HEM

1. Create a narrow turned hem on the Skirt Drape (E) along the longest edge. To do this, turn hem under ¼" (6 mm) and press. Turn under again ⅜" (1 cm) and stitch to form a narrow hem. Alternately, use a rolled hem foot on your sewing machine, which will create a very small, tightly rolled hem. (Figure 6)

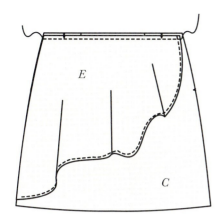

FIGURE 7

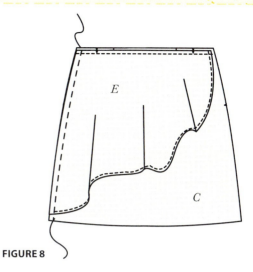

FIGURE 8

ATTACH SKIRT DRAPE

1. With right sides facing up, pin Skirt Drape (E) to Skirt Front (C) at the waist, matching the notches.

2. Machine baste the Skirt Drape (E) to the Skirt Front (C) at the waist. (Figure 7)

3. Pin Skirt Drape (E) to Skirt Front (C) at the side seam, matching the notches.

4. Machine baste the Skirt Drape (E) to the Skirt Front (C) at the side. (Figure 8)

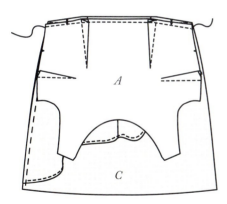

FIGURE 9

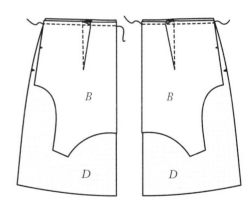

FIGURE 10

JOIN BODICE FRONT TO SKIRT FRONT

1. With right sides together, pin Bodice Front (A) to Skirt Front (C) at the waist, matching notches. Stitch. (Figure 9)

2. Press seam toward the bodice.

JOIN BODICE BACK TO SKIRT BACK

1. With right sides together, pin Bodice Back (B) pieces to Skirt Back (D) pieces at the waist. Stitch. (Figure 10)

2. Press seams toward the bodice.

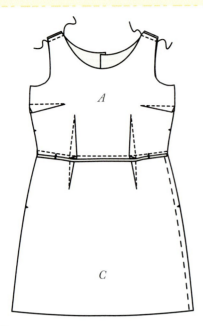

FIGURE 11

SEW SHOULDER SEAMS

1. With right sides together, stitch Bodice Front (A) to Bodice Back (B) pieces at the shoulder seams. (Figure 11)

2. Finish seams and press open.

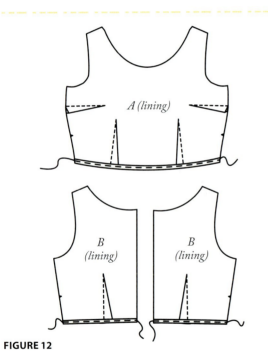

FIGURE 12

BASTE WAIST LINING

1. Turn the waistline edge of each bodice lining piece under ½" (1.3 cm) and baste. (Figure 12)

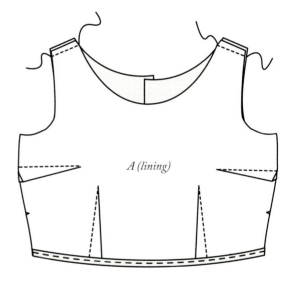

FIGURE 13

SEW LINING SHOULDER SEAMS

1. With right sides together, stitch Bodice Front (A) lining to Bodice Back (B) lining pieces at the shoulder seams. (Figure 13)

2. Finish seams and press open.

ATTACH BODICE LINING

1. With right sides together, lay the bodice lining over the bodice shell, aligning all of the edges at both the front and the back. Pin in place along the neckline and armholes.

2. Stitch the lining to the bodice at the armholes. (Figure 14)

3. Trim the seam allowance, and clip the inner curves.

4. Stitch the lining to the bodice at the neckline, stopping about 1½" to 2" (3.9-5.1 cm) from the center back. This will leave you enough room to install the zipper.

5. Trim the seam allowance, clip the inner curves and understitch.

6. Turn the entire dress right-side out by pulling the dress through one of the shoulders. You may want to use a sharp object, such as a knitting needle, to help push fabric through the narrow passage. (Figure 15)

7. Press the neckline and armholes.

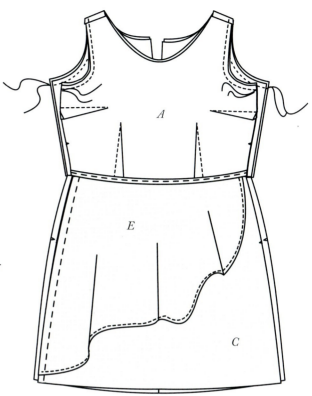

FIGURE 14

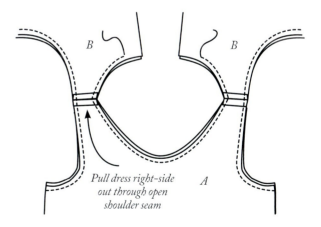

Pull dress right-side out through open shoulder seam

FIGURE 15

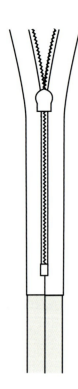

FIGURE 16

SEW IN ZIPPER

1. Open the lining away from the shell of the dress.

2. Using an invisible zipper foot, sew in the invisible zipper above the large circle.

3. Stitch the center back seam closed below the zipper and press open. (Figure 16)

4. Now that the zipper is sewn to the outside of the dress, turn the dress and finish the 1½" to 2" inches (3.9-5.1 cm) that you left unstitched at the back neckline.

5. With the wrong side of the lining facing you, stitch the lining to the zipper tape, taking care not to sew through the dress. Do this on both sides of the zipper. See pages 144-145 for instructions on sewing a lining to a zipper.

6. Hand sew the hook and eye at the back neck opening, above the zipper, on the inside of the dress.

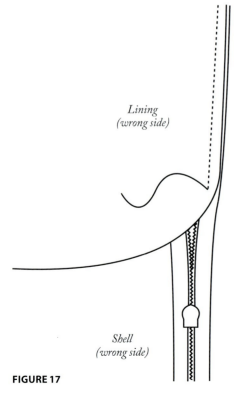

Lining (wrong side)

Shell (wrong side)

FIGURE 17

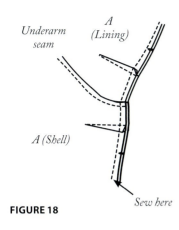

FIGURE 18

SEW THE SIDE SEAMS

1. Open the bodice lining away from the shell. You will now sew each side seam in one continuous seam.

2. Pin the Bodice Front (A) lining to the Bodice Back (B) lining pieces at the side seams. Pin the dress shell front to the back at the side seams. Make sure to align all of the matching seams, including the underarm seams.

3. Stitch the left bodice lining side seam and shell side seam in one continuous seam. (Figure 18) Repeat for the right side.

4. Finish the seams and press open.

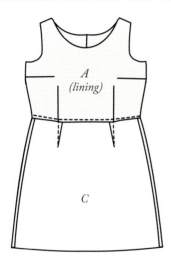

FIGURE 19

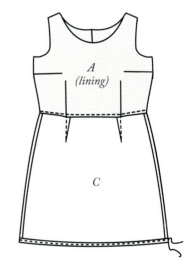

FIGURE 20

STITCH BODICE LINING WAIST

1. On the inside of the dress, baste the bodice lining to the waist, making sure that the bodice lining covers the waist seam. (Figure 19)

2. Turn the dress right side out.

3. Stitch in the ditch along the waist seam to join the bodice lining to the dress at the waist. Alternately, you can slipstitch the lining to the waist by hand (see page 17). Remove the basting stitches and press.

SEW HEMS

1. On the skirt, turn hem under ¼" (6 mm) and press.

2. Turn under again ⅜" (1 cm) and stitch to form a narrow hem. (Figure 20)

Chapter Six

A FINE FINISH

When you look at a garment to see how well it's made, the first place you look is probably the seams. When a dress or blouse looks as neat and lovely on the inside as it does on the outside, it tells you that the maker really cared enough to do things right. In some cases, these interior finishes might be visible to the outside world, such as in a sheer blouse or when you flash the lining of a coat. Other times, you might be the only one to see the insides. Even then, if you take the time to make it well, you'll notice that you have a different perspective on your finished projects. They will feel special, more handmade than homemade. I believe good finishing is the hallmark of a garment that is made with love.

Once you get in the habit of finishing, seams that are left unfinished and raw will start to feel messy and incomplete. But that's not the only reason to learn about finishing techniques. Finishing raw edges will also extend the life of your garment, keeping the cut edges of your fabric from raveling and possibly destroying the integrity of your seams.

For me, the best reason to create handmade clothing is to make yourself something special, something that you will love. Even if you can't afford to buy expensive designer clothing, you can afford to make yourself the best if you take a slow and considered approach. Treat yourself to a garment that feels as lovely and detailed on the inside as it does on the outside.

SEAM FINISHES

There are many techniques for finishing seams, but the goal of each is to treat the raw edges of your fabric to prevent raveling and give a neat appearance. You should choose a method that's appropriate for the fabric you are using and the type of garment you are making.

BOUND EDGE

This is a method of finishing an edge, such as a neckline or sleeve hem, by enclosing it with bias tape. The seam allowance will vary, depending on the size of the bias tape you use. Use a bound edge when your pattern calls for one, such as the Taffy Blouse pattern in this chapter. You can purchase bias tape, or make your own (see pages 138–139).

1. Open out the bias tape and, with right sides together, align the raw edges of the tape and the garment and pin around the edge. If you're binding a circular opening, such as a neckline, leave enough tape to overlap the ends by a few inches.

2. Stitch around the edge along the first fold line, stopping a few inches from the overlap on each side.

3. Join the tape together at the overlap, leaving enough room to stitch the tape to those remaining few inches.

4. Trim off the excess and press the seam open.

5. Finish stitching the few inches you left open to complete the circle of stitching.

6. Fold the tape over the raw edge, folding all the raw edges within the binding. Pin in place from the front.

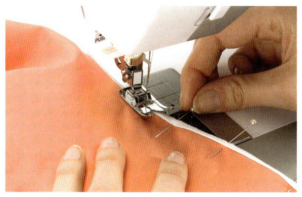

7. Edgestitch along the fold from the front, catching the other side of the binding in the stitching.

DESIGNING WITH BIAS TAPE

Bias tape is one of my favorite design elements. It gives you a neat and professional finish, but it can also be used for decorative effect.

You can make bias tape using your main fabric for a polished, simple look, or you can purchase or make bias tape in a contrasting color. (If using patterned fabrics, choose very small-scale patterns, so they'll be visible on narrow bindings.)

In addition to binding edges, bias tape can be sandwiched into a seam to create a flat sort of piping, or it can be stitched right onto the surface of your clothing! Because it stretches and bends and curves, you can use it in limitless ways to decorate the things you make.

MAKING BIAS TAPE

Though you can purchase ready-made bias tape, making your own greatly increases the range of fabrics, colors and patterns you can incorporate into your sewing. Making bias tape from your garment fabric will give you a particularly clean and professional finish, or you can make beautifully patterned or contrasting tapes for almost any project. I recommend a small inexpensive tool called a bias tape maker, which comes in different sizes and helps you fold your edges perfectly. Use natural fabrics, since they hold a crease well when pressed.

1. Cut out a square of fabric. Fold it in half diagonally, from corner to corner, so that it creases. Cut along the fold line.

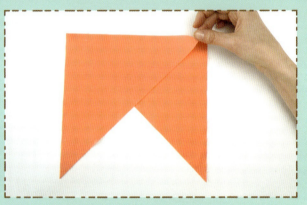

2. Lay the two pieces right sides together as shown, and pin.

3. Sew the two pieces together, as shown in the diagram, using a ¼" (6 mm) seam allowance.

4. Press the seam open.

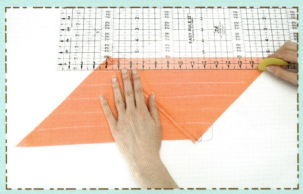

5. With a ruler and tailor's chalk, draw lines as shown on the wrong side, measuring so the width of each strip is twice the final width of your binding. For ½" (1.3 cm) binding, mark 1" (2.5 cm) strips.

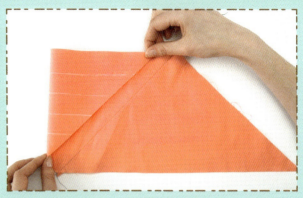

6. Fold inward to create a rectangle, with the first line offset on each side.

7. Align the lines and, with right sides together, pin in place.

8. Stitch with a ¼" (6 mm) seam allowance and press open.

9. Begin cutting on the first line and continue cutting in one long continuous strip.

10. Feed the end through a bias tape maker and slowly pull the strip through, pressing the folds flat as the tape emerges. If you don't have a bias tape maker, you can just fold the edges in to meet at the center, and press. The bias tape maker simply folds it for you. For double fold bias tape, fold the tape in half again when you are done and press once more.

FRENCH SEAM

A French seam is sewn twice, encasing the raw edges within the seam. It creates a very neat, narrow seam, making it perfect for sheer or very light fabrics. It's not suited for heavy fabrics, since it will create too much bulk.

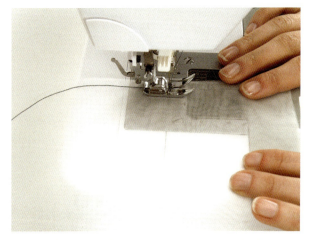

1. With wrong sides together, stitch using a ¼" (6 mm) seam allowance.

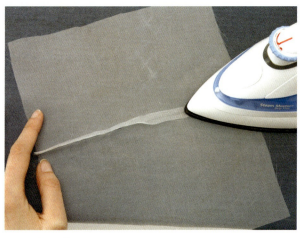

2. Press the seam as it was sewn, and then press it open.

3. Fold the fabric around the seam with right sides together, creasing along the seamline, and press.

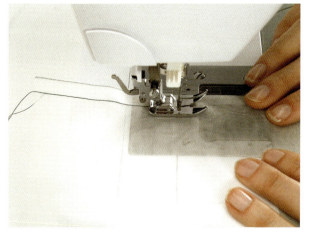

4. Stitch using a ⅜" (1 cm) seam allowance, encasing the raw edge within the seam. Press to one side.

FLAT FELLED SEAM

Flat felled seams are quite strong and are found often in tailored shirts or trousers. Take a look at your favorite jeans and you'll find flat felled seams. Use this technique when extra strength or durability is needed. There are several ways to create flat felled seams, but this is the most basic.

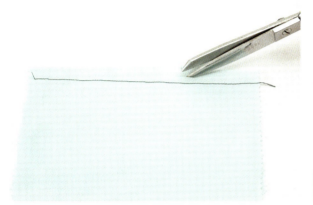

1. After stitching the usual ⅝" (1.6 cm) seam, trim one side of the seam allowance to just ¼" (6 mm).

2. Fold the other side of the allowance over, aligning the raw edge with the stitching.

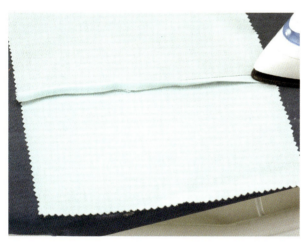

3. Fold the whole seam over again along the stitching line, and press.

4. Edgestitch the seam allowance.

BOUND SEAM

A bound seam uses binding around the raw edges of a stitched seam. Because of its bulk, it can show through on lighter fabrics, so it's most often used with very sturdy fabrics such as denim, or on jackets and outerwear. It's a wonderful opportunity to use a fun color or printed binding, to add some flash to the inside of your garment.

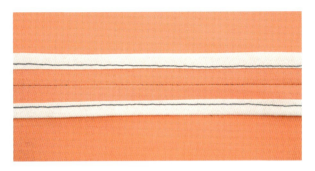

After stitching your seam, press open and use the binding method on page 136 to bind each raw edge of the seam separately.

SERGED SEAM

Serging is what you will see most often in ready-to-wear clothing. Raw edges are stitched with a special machine called a serger, which holds multiple spools of thread and trims the seams as it sews. If you don't have a serger, you can try zigzag stitching over the raw edges of your seam allowance, or use your sewing machine's overlock stitch if it has one. Be aware that this uses a considerable amount of thread.

After stitching your seam, serge over the edges of the seam allowance either separately or together.

PINKED SEAM

Pinked seams are simple to create, requiring just a pair of pinking shears. The zigzag pattern of the cut edge keeps the fabric from raveling. Pinked seams are commonly found within vintage garments, which goes to show that they can last. Use pinked seams on cottons and other somewhat sturdy fabrics that are not very prone to fraying.

After sewing a seam, trim the seam using pinking shears. Press the seam as directed in the pattern.

LINING

Even if your pattern does not include a lining, it can be a beautiful addition to many garments. Linings can help a garment drape better over the body, skimming gently over curves and bulges. They hide the inside of seams, so that finishing raw edges isn't necessary. They can also make garments more comfortable, and help the garment to wrinkle less. The lining is usually attached the facing. If I am adding a lining to a pattern that doesn't have one, I like to cut the lining from the garment pattern pieces, then stitch the facing right over the lining to create a single unit. This method is quick, doesn't involve making new pattern pieces, and the lining fabric can act as interfacing underneath the facing.

LINING FABRICS

You can choose from a wide array of fabrics for lining garments, but look for fabrics with drape and smoothness. Be sure that the lining fabric has the same care requirements that your outer fabric has.

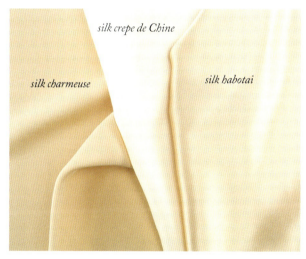

Lightweight Silks

Lightweight silks are my absolute favorite for lining, because they are comfortable, breathable, soft and come in gorgeous colors and prints. Silk charmeuse is exceptionally lovely, as is crepe de Chine. Habotai is the most lightweight, which makes it very comfortable.

Lining-Specific Fabrics

In addition to natural silks, there are many lining-specific fabrics available. Bemberg is one of the best, because it's breathable and easy to wash in the machine. Hang Loose is a polyester lining, so while it looks nice, it's not as comfortable to wear. Acetate is very inexpensive, but harder to work with and not very comfortable to wear.

ADD A LINING

Sometimes it makes sense to add a lining, even if your pattern doesn't call for one. If your fabric is sheer, a lining will make your garment wearable without a separate slip. A lining also allows clothes to glide over your body easily, so it's great when a fabric feels too clingy. For this demonstration, I'm using organza for the lining so that you can see the layers, but I don't recommend it for real linings. See the previous page for details on lining fabrics.

1. To add a free-hanging lining to a dress, blouse or skirt, the easiest method is to cut the lining fabric from your garment pattern pieces. On most dresses and blouses, sleeves are usually not lined.

2. On your facing pieces, turn in the lower edges to form a hem and press. Lay the facing pieces over the matching lining pieces with right sides up, and stitch the facing right on top of the lining. Assemble the lining just as you do the garment, then install the facing/lining when your instructions tell you to add the facing. Flip, then press the seam.

LINING AND ZIPPERS

If your garment has a zipper, it's much easier than it seems to attach the lining to it. This works best with an invisible zipper, because it's not topstitched to the garment.

1. Install the zipper in the garment before you attach the lining. Here, I am pressing the invisible zipper after sewing it in place.

2. Assemble the lining, leaving an opening in the seam where the zipper will be. Press this entire seam open.

3. With right sides together, attach the lining to the garment. In this case, the lining is joined to the garment at the neckline. If the seam is curved, like this neckline, clip the seam allowance after sewing.

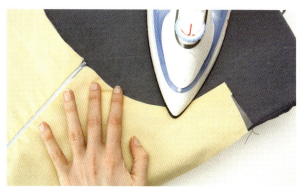

4. Flip right-side-out, and press the seam.

5. Once the lining is installed with wrong sides together, reach between the lining layer and the garment and grasp one side's seam allowance where the zipper is attached. Also grasp the lining seam allowance.

6. Turn the seam to the outside and pin the lining to the zipper seam.

7. Stitch the lining to the seam allowance.

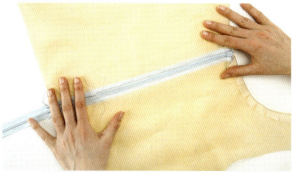

8. Repeat steps 5 through 7 for the other side. Press.

Project

TAFFY BLOUSE

This beautiful, floating blouse with flutter sleeves combines a few techniques you may not have tried before. It is cut on the bias, allowing it to stretch and conform gently to the body's curves. It also employs two finishing techniques. First, the blouse is constructed with French seams, so you are free to use a sheer fabric without worrying about messy fraying showing through. Second, the neckline and sleeve hems are bound with bias tape. On the neckline, this eliminates the need for a facing, which would show through and look unattractive with a sheer fabric. At the sleeve hems, it means you don't have to turn the hem under, which would be extremely difficult on a hem that is this curved. For more about these finishing techniques, review the bias tape and French seams techniques earlier in this chapter.

Try making your own bias tape and using it as a design element. You can do a solid blouse with bias tape in a print, like this one, or do a printed blouse with coordinating solid binding. Making bias tape is also a great way to reuse old clothing that no longer fits or salvage fabric from secondhand store finds. In fact, the black and white silk bias tape here was made from an old silk button-down shirt. You'd be surprised how much tape you can get out of an old piece of clothing!

(The skirt in this photo is the Meringue Skirt pattern from pages 52-59.)

TOOLS

sewing shears (or rotary cutter and mat)
pattern weights
pins
hand sewing needle
marking pen or chalk

SUPPLIES

fabric (see Fabric Suggestions and Fabric Required table)
thread
5½ yards (5 meters) of ½" (1.3 cm) double fold bias tape (purchased or made from your own fabric)

SKILLS CHECKLIST

* *Preparing your fabric (pp. 42–43)*
* *Laying out your pattern (pp. 44–45)*
* *Cutting out your pattern (pp. 50–51)*
* *Transferring the markings (pp. 48–49)*
* *Fitting a muslin (pp. 73-76)*
* *Choosing a fabric (pp. 104-107)*
* *Making bias tape (pp. 138-139)*
* *Sewing darts (pp. 20-21)*
* *Sewing French seams (p. 140)*
* *Binding edges with bias tape (pp. 136-137)*

FABRIC SUGGESTIONS

This blouse is designed for a lightweight fabric, and the French seams make even the sheerest fabrics look perfect. Chiffon, georgette, lawn or silk charmeuse are good choices.

FABRIC REQUIRED (YARDS AND METERS):

To find your size, check the size chart at the end of the book.

	0	2	4	6	8	10	12	14	16	18
FABRIC, 45" (115 CM)	1⅝ yards (1.5 m)	1⅝ yards (1.5 m)	1¾ yards (1.6 m)	1¾ yards (1.6 m)	1¾ yards (1.6 m)	1⅞ yards (1.7 m)	1⅞ yards (1.7 m)	1⅞ yards (1.7 m)	1⅞ yards (1.7 m)	2 yards (1.8 m)
FABRIC, 60" (150 CM)	1⅜ yards (1.3 m)	1⅜ yards (1.3 m)	1½ yards (1.4 m)	1½ yards (1.4 m)	1½ yards (1.4 m)	1⅝ yards (1.5 m)	1⅝ yards (1.5 m)	1⅝ yards (1.5 m)	1⅝ yards (1.5 m)	1⅔ yards (1.6 m)

FINISHED GARMENT MEASUREMENTS (INCHES):

	0	2	4	6	8	10	12	14	16	18
BUST	36" (91 cm)	37" (94 cm)	38" (97 cm)	39" (99 cm)	40" (102 cm)	41½" (105 cm)	42" (107 cm)	44 " (112 cm)	46" (117 cm)	48" (123 cm)
BACK LENGTH*	22" (56 cm)	22½ " (57 cm)	23" (58 cm)	23½" (60 cm)	24" (61 cm)	24½ " (62 cm)	25" (64 cm)	25½ " (65 cm)	26" (66 cm)	26½ (67 cm)
HEM WIDTH	36" (91 cm)	37" (94 cm)	38" (97 cm)	39" (99 cm)	40" (102 cm)	41½ (105 cm)	43" (107 cm)	45" (112 cm)	46" (117 cm)	48" (123 cm)

* Back length is measured from the base of your neck to the hem.

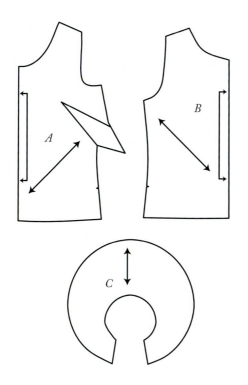

PATTERN INVENTORY

A - Blouse Front
B - Blouse Back
C - Sleeve

All pieces include ⅝" (1.6 cm) seam allowance.

CUTTING LAYOUTS

Fabric most frequently comes in widths of 45" (115 cm) or 60" (150 cm), but widths do vary. Your cutting layout may also need to change for a napped or one-way fabric (see page 44 for details), or you may need a different layout for matching stripes or plaids (see pages 46-47). The striped area is the wrong side of the pattern pieces; flip the pattern over along the center fold line to create one piece.

FABRIC, 45" (115 CM):

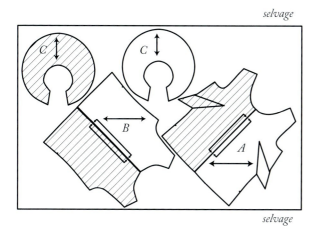

FABRIC, 60" (150 CM), SIZES 0 TO 14:

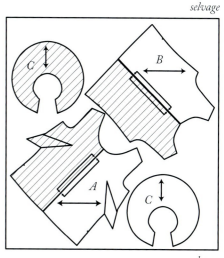

INSTRUCTIONS

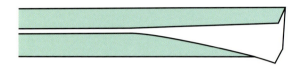

FIGURE 1

MAKE BIAS TAPE

1. Begin by making the bias tape listed under "supplies," if you are not using purchased bias tape. See pages 138-139, for instructions on making bias tape. (Figure 1)

FIGURE 2

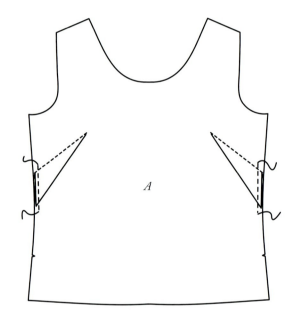

FIGURE 3

SEW DARTS

1. On Blouse Front (A) pieces, bring the legs of each dart together and pin. Stitch darts and tie off the ends. (Figure 2)

PRESS AND BASTE DARTS

1. Press the darts toward the waist.

2. At the sides of Blouse Front (A), align the raw edges of the dart to the raw edge of the side seam and baste in place. This will ensure that the dart is caught neatly in the French seam later on, leaving no raw edges. (Figure 3)

SEW SHOULDER SEAMS

1. Starting with wrong sides together, pin Blouse Front (A) to Blouse Back (B) at the shoulders.

2. Sew the shoulders together using a French seam. For complete step-by-step instructions on sewing a French seam, see page 140. (Figure 4)

3. Press the shoulder seams toward the back.

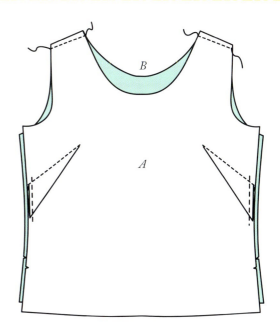

FIGURE 4

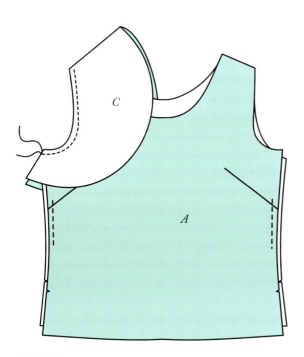

FIGURE 5

ATTACH SLEEVES

1. With a French seamed garment, the sleeves are joined to the garment before the side seams are sewn, so that the sleeves can be sewn flat. Starting with the wrong sides together, pin each Sleeve (C) to the armholes, matching notches and aligning the large circle with the shoulder seam.

2. Sew each Sleeve (C) to the armhole using a French seam. (Figure 5)

3. Press each seam toward the blouse.

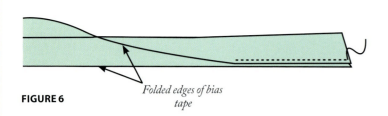

FIGURE 6

Folded edges of bias tape

CREATE WAIST TIES

1. Create waist ties by cutting two 24" (61 cm) lengths of bias tape.

2. Fold each in half along the length so that the raw edges are encased in the middle, and press.

3. Edgestitch the waist ties down the length. (Figure 6)

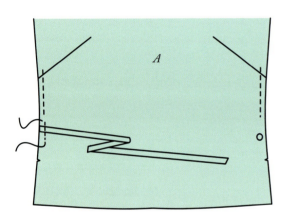

FIGURE 7

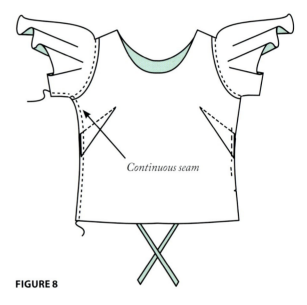

Continuous seam

FIGURE 8

ATTACH WAIST TIES

1. On the right side of Blouse Front (A), position one waist tie over each of the two small circles on the side seams, aligning the raw edges.

2. Baste ties into place at the waist. (Figure 7)

3. Tie a single knot at the end of each waist tie and trim close to the knot for a decorative finish.

SEW SIDE SEAMS

1. With wrong sides together, pin Blouse Front (A) to Blouse Back (B) at the side seams, matching notches and underarm seam. Pin each Sleeve (C) together at the underarm seam.

2. Sew the entire side seam using a French seam, sewing all the way through the underarm to the Sleeve (C) hem in a continuous seam. (Figure 8)

3. Press the seam toward the back.

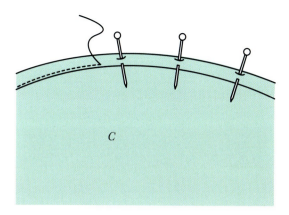

FIGURE 9

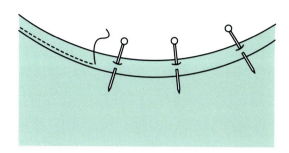

FIGURE 10

BIND SLEEVE HEMS

1. Finish the hem of each Sleeve (C) piece by binding the raw edge of the hem with bias tape. While a traditional turned hem would be very difficult on a deep curve, such as this, the stretch of the bias tape easily conforms around the hem. For complete step-by-step instructions on binding with bias tape including joining the ends together, see pages 136-137.

BIND NECKLINE

1. Bind around the entire neckline with bias tape, joining the ends of the bias tape as shown on pages 136-137.

FIGURE 11

HEM THE BLOUSE

1. Use a narrow hem to finish the lower edge of the blouse. Begin by turning the lower edge under ¼" (6mm) and press.

2. Turn the edge under again ⅜" (1 cm) and press. Stitch the hem in place by edgestitching close to the first fold. (Figure 11)

Chapter Seven

KEEP LEARNING

*M*y approach to learning is simple: Take it one skill at a time.

Choose projects that you can handle, but that stretch your limits a little bit. Think about the skills you want to acquire or improve when it comes to sewing, then choose your sewing projects accordingly. If you want to learn more about tailoring, try making a tailored jacket. It you're interested in learning more about linings, make a lined skirt or dress.

The other part of this approach is research. Most newer sewers learn by trial and error and working with commercial patterns. The truth is, most patterns will only teach you the most basic methods, not necessarily the best or even the easiest for every sewer. While Colette Patterns are a little different in this regard, with more emphasis on instruction, every pattern is bound to be somewhat limited by space and in order to appeal to a wide audience of different skill levels.

Instead of just following pattern instructions, combine your instructions with a little independent research. Look for books that might show you new and interesting ways to do things, then apply those skills. Search online for tips and tricks that can improve your sewing. Check out sewing blogs and follow along with what others are doing. Join sewing communities, like the one at colettepatterns.com, to learn from other sewers and get feedback and advice.

Remember that more than anything else, your own curiosity is what will make you an adventurous and skilled seamstress.

RECOMMENDED READING

Sewing is a complex skill, which is what makes it so engrossing to many of us. There is always more to learn. To help you along the way, begin building up your own home sewing library.

GENERAL REFERENCE

You should have one or more basic reference books to guide you along the nuts and bolts of sewing.

Vogue Sewing
A classic sewing book that covers many techniques in detail.

Readers Digest New Complete Guide to Sewing
An easy-to-follow reference for the true beginner.

The Sewing Bible: A Modern Manual of Practical and Decorative Sewing Techniques
Ruth Singer
A wonderfully comprehensive sewing manual, with several simple projects included.

The Dressmaking Book: A Simplified Guide for Beginners
Adele P. Margolis
This is an older book by an incomparable sewing teacher and writer. Adele Margolis provides clear instruction and plenty of detail. Each of her books is worth looking for!

TECHNIQUES

When you want to really dive into a sewing topic, such as getting a good fit or sewing on the bias, look for more specific technique books. These will be more focused and allow you to dig deep on the topic you're interested in.

FITTING

Pattern Fitting With Confidence
Nancy Zieman
Nancy Zieman guides you through a clear process of fitting patterns to your own body.

The Perfect Fit: The Classic Guide to Altering Patterns
Editors of Creative Publishing
Another concise and clearly written book on fitting.

Fit for Real People: Sew Great Clothes Using ANY Pattern (Sewing for Real People series)
Pati Palmer, Marta Alto
Covers the concept of tissue fitting, from start to finish.

FABRIC

Claire Shaeffer's Fabric Sewing Guide
Claire Shaeffer
An amazing reference for helping you understand and choose fabric.

More Fabric Savvy: A Quick Resource Guide to Selecting and Sewing Fabric
Sandra Betzina
Another useful and comprehensive guide for understanding fabric and how to use it.

SPECIFIC TECHNIQUES

When you want to really dive into a sewing topic, look for more specific technique books. These will be more focused and allow you to dig deep on the topic you're interested in.

The Art of Manipulating Fabric
Colette Wolff
One of my all-time favorite sewing books. Even with simple black and white photography, this book will inspire you with pages and pages of ideas for creating interesting details with fabric.

Easy Guide to Sewing Linings
Connie Long
A wonderful and concise guide on adding linings to practically any garment.

Making Trousers for Men & Women
David Page Coffin
When you set out to learn to make a pair of really great trousers, keep this book handy and you won't be disappointed!

Shirtmaking
David Page Coffin
Another wonderfully detailed book, this time on the art of shirtmaking

Tailoring: The Classic Guide to Sewing the Perfect Jacket
Editors of Creative Publishing
Indispensable guide for turning your simple jackets and coats into works of true tailoring.

Couture Sewing Techniques
By Claire Shaeffer
Explains many of the more advanced techniques that go into making a truly exceptional couture garment, including a great deal of information on hand sewing.

WEBSITES

The Coletterie: www.colettepatterns.com/blog
This is the Colette Patterns sewing blog! Our team writes all about fashion history, classic sewing techniques, vintage inspiration, and plenty of tutorials and free projects to try. Stop by to say hi in our forum!

The Sew Weekly: www.sewweekly.com
Founded by Mena Trott, *The Sew Weekly* challenges everyone involved to sew a new garment every week. With a thriving and supportive community, this is one of the most inspiring sewing blogs out there.

Pattern Review: sewing.patternreview.com
This large community website includes sewers at all levels of expertise. As the name suggests, there are countless reviews for sewing patterns, but there are also active forums, classes, live chat sessions and more!

A Fashionable Stitch: www.afashionablestitch.com
Sunni shares tips and ideas, along with her own fabulous projects. Look for sew-alongs and great information for beginners, along with a lot of project inspiration.

Sew Mama Sew!: sewmamasew.com
A popular blog that covers all manner of sewing, from garments to crafts and quilts. You'll find a range of amazing tutorials and projects here.

Casey's Elegant Musings: elegantmusings.com
Casey has an elegant vintage style that shines through in everything she makes. Beautiful projects, sew-alongs and ideas abound on this sweet and welcoming blog.

Flossie Teacakes: flossieteacakes.blogspot.com
Florence is a talented sewing writer with a sweet vintage aesthetic. She dreams up lovely patterns and tutorials that will have you pulling out your needle and thread with a side of tea.

Gertie's New Blog for Better Sewing:
www.blogforbettersewing.com
Gertie is a force to be reckoned with! Author, sewing teacher and lover of vintage style, she has a passion for teaching classic techniques.

Angry Chicken:
angrychicken.typepad.com/angry_chicken
Sewing and craft author Amy Karol writes a personal/craft blog that I've been reading and loving for many years. Her wonderful personality, sense of humor and inviting teaching style make this blog a must-visit.

Fehr Trade: www.fehrtrade.com
Melissa Fehr is a self-taught seamstress who documents her sewing beautifully. She includes many reviews of European pattern magazines and renders her own unique versions of these fashionable patterns.

Tilly and the Buttons: www.tillyandthebuttons.com
One of the things that sets Tilly apart as a sewing blogger is that she is fairly new to sewing. But that doesn't stop her from making incredible vintage-inspired garments. Follow along with this talented lady!

Project

LICORICE DRESS

$\mathcal{T}$he licorice dress is a short and sweet little frock that just skims over the curves of the body. The all-in-one construction of the bodice and skirt make it fairly easy to sew, so take your time getting the fit just the way you want it. A light lining helps the dress glide gracefully over the body. The wide collar is tucked at the back and shoulders to give it an interesting drape. The sleeves are full, ending in elasticized gathers just above the elbow. The elastic casing that finishes the sleeve hems is made from bias tape, giving you a perfect opportunity to try your hand at making your own from your dress fabric.

This is your chance to combine all the principles from this book to make yourself something really lovely. Begin by sketching out ideas and deciding on an overall look for the dress. Use your fabric knowledge to pick out a suitable fabric with the right amount of weight and drape. Read the pattern carefully and work with it to prepare and cut your muslin for fitting. Once you have the fit just the way you want it, create your custom dress, using the bias tape and lining to give a professional finish.

(To see this dress sewn using an alternate fabric, refer to page 1.)

TOOLS

sewing shears (or rotary cutter and mat)
pattern weights
pins
hand sewing needle
marking pen or chalk
invisible zipper presser foot
safety pin (optional)
pinking shears (optional)
bamboo point turner (optional)

SUPPLIES

shell fabric (see Fabric Suggestions and Fabric Required table)
lining fabric (see Fabric Suggestions and Fabric Required table)
thread
2 yards (1.8 m) of ½" (1.3 cm) bias tape (purchased, or made from the shell fabric)
1 yard (.9 m) of ⅜" (1 cm) elastic
24" (61 cm) invisible zipper
one small hook and eye closure

SKILLS CHECKLIST

*Preparing your fabric (pp. 42–43)
* Laying out your pattern (pp. 44–45)
*Cutting out your pattern (pp. 50-51)
*Transferring the markings (pp. 48–49)
* Sewing darts (pp. 20–21)
* Sewing double-pointed darts (p. 21)
*Pressing a seam (p. 18)
* Setting a sleeve (p.26)
* Sewing an invisible zipper (p. 23)
* Sewing a lining with a zipper (pp. 144–145)

FABRIC REQUIRED (YARDS AND METERS):

To find your size, check the size chart at the end of the book.

	0	2	4	6	8	10	12	14	16	18
SHELL FABRIC, 45" (115 CM)	3¼ yard (3 m)	3⅜ yards (3.1 m)	3⅜ yards (3.1 m)	3½ yards (3.2 m)	3½ yards (3.2 m)	3¾ yards (3.4 m)	3¾ yards (3.4 m)	3¾ yards (3.4 m)	3⅞ yards (3.5 m)	3⅞ yards (3.5 m)
SHELL FABRIC, 60" (150 CM)	2⅞ yards (2.6 m)	2⅞ yards (2.6 m)	3 yards (2.7 m)	3 yards (2.7 m)	3 yards (2.7 m)	3⅛ yard (2.9 m)	3⅛ yard (2.9 m)	3⅛ yard (2.9 m)	3¼ yard (3 m)	3¼ yard (3 m)
LINING FABRIC, 45" (115 CM)	2 yards (1.8m)	2 yards (1.8m)	2⅛ yards (2m)	2⅛ yards (2m)	2⅛ yards (2m)	2¼ yards (2.1m)	2¼ yards (2.1m)	2¼ yards (2.1m)	2⅓ yards (2.1m)	2⅓ yards (2.1m)
LINING FABRIC, 60" (150 CM)	1¾ yards (1.6m)	1¾ yards (1.6m)	1⅞ yards (1.7m)	1⅞ yards (1.7m)	1⅞ yards (1.7m)	2 yards (1.8m)	2 yards (1.8m)	2 yards (1.8m)	2⅛ yards (2m)	2⅛ yards (2m)

FINISHED GARMENT MEASUREMENTS (INCHES):

	0	2	4	6	8	10	12	14	16	18
BACK LENGTH*	36" (91 cm)	36½" (93 cm)	37" (94 cm)	37½" (95 cm)	38" (97 cm)	38½" (98 cm)	39" (99 cm)	39½" (100 cm)	40" (102 cm)	40½" (103 cm)
HEM WIDTH	45" (114 cm)	46" (117 cm)	47" (119 cm)	48" (122 cm)	49" (124 cm)	50½" (128 cm)	52" (132 cm)	55" (140 cm)	57" (145 cm)	59" (150 cm)
BUST	36" (91 cm)	37" (94 cm)	38" (97 cm)	39" (99 cm)	40" (102 cm)	41½" (103 cm)	43" (109 cm)	45" (114 cm)	47" (119 cm)	49" (124 cm)
WAIST	28⅞" (73 cm)	29⅞" (76 cm)	30⅞" (78 cm)	31⅞" (81 cm)	32⅞" (84 cm)	34⅜" (87 cm)	35⅞" (91 cm)	37⅞" (96 cm)	39⅞" (101 cm)	41⅞" (106 cm)
HIP	40" (102 cm)	41" (104 cm)	42" (107 cm)	43" (109 cm)	44" (112 cm)	45½" (114 cm)	47" (119 cm)	49" (124 cm)	51" (130 cm)	53" (135 cm)

* Back length is measured from the base of your neck to the hem.

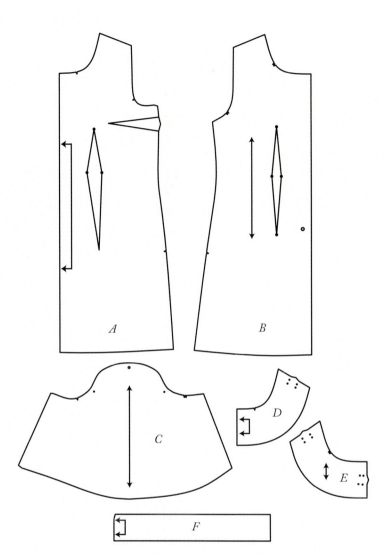

PATTERN INVENTORY

A - Dress Front

B - Dress Back

C - Sleeve

D - Collar Front (one for sizes 0-8; one for sizes 10-18)

E - Collar Back (one for sizes 0-8; one for sizes 10-18)

F - Tie Belt

All pieces include ⅝" (1.6 cm) seam allowance.

FABRIC SUGGESTIONS

Choose a soft fabric that drapes well for this dress. Lightweight fabrics with drape, such as silk or rayon crepe, charmeuse, lawn, voile or wool crepe work well. For the lining, choose a lightweight fabric, such as silk habotai or Bemberg rayon.

CUTTING LAYOUTS

Fabric most frequently comes in widths of 45" (115 cm) or 60" (150 cm), but widths do vary. Your cutting layout may also need to change for a napped or one-way fabric (see page 44 for details), or you may need a different layout for matching stripes or plaids (see pages 46-47). The striped area is the wrong side of the pattern pieces.

SHELL FABRIC, 45" (115 CM):

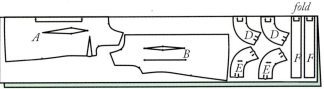

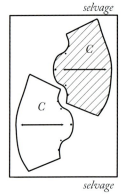

SHELL FABRIC, 60" (150 CM), SIZES 0 TO 14:

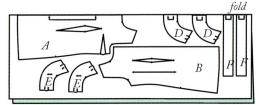

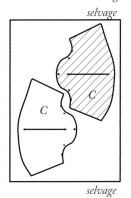

LINING FABRIC, 45" (115 CM), SIZES 0 TO 14:

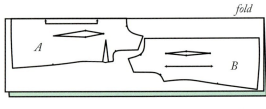

LINING FABRIC, 60" (150 CM), SIZES 0 TO 14:

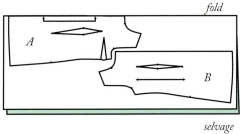

INSTRUCTIONS

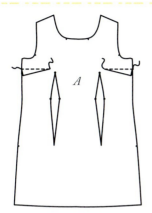

FIGURE 1

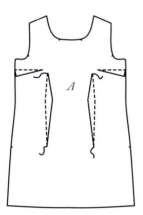

FIGURE 2

SEW FRONT DARTS

1. On Dress Front (A), bring the legs of the horizontal side bust darts together and pin. Stitch darts and tie off ends.

2. Press the darts down, toward the waist. (Figure 1)

3. Bring the legs of the double-pointed center darts together and pin.

4. Stitch darts, beginning at the center of each dart and stitching toward the first point. Return to the center and stitch to the second point. Tie off ends.

5. Press darts toward center. (Figure 2)

SEW BACK DARTS

1. On each Dress Back (B) piece, bring the legs of the double-pointed center darts together and pin.

2. Stitch darts, beginning at the center of each dart and stitching toward the first point. Return to the center and stitch to the second point. Tie off ends.

3. Press darts toward center back edges. (Figure 3) See page 21 for more on sewing double-pointed darts.

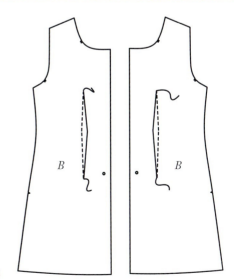

FIGURE 3

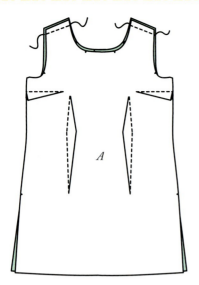

FIGURE 4

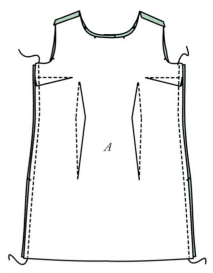

FIGURE 5

SEW SHOULDER SEAMS

1. With right sides together, stitch Dress Front (A) and Dress Back (B) together at the shoulders. (Figure 4)

2. Press shoulder seams open.

3. Staystitch around the neckline to prevent stretching.

SEW SIDE SEAMS

1. With right sides together, stitch Dress Front (A) to Dress Back (B) pieces at the side seams. (Figure 5)

2. Press side seams open.

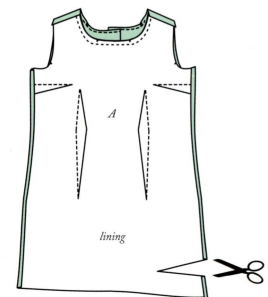

FIGURE 6

SEW DRESS LINING

1. To create the lining, follow all of the previous steps using the Dress Front (A) lining and Dress Back (B) lining pieces.

2. Trim 1½" (3.8 cm) from the hem of the lining, so that the lining will remain shorter than the dress shell. (Figure 6)

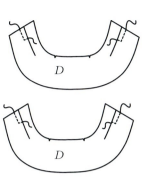
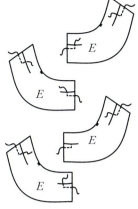
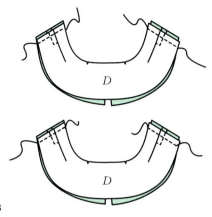

FIGURE 7

FIGURE 8

CREATE COLLAR TUCKS

1. To create tucks in the Collar Front (D) and Collar Back (E) pieces, bring large circles to meet small circles with right sides together, and pin.

2. Stitch each tuck between circles, pivoting at the end of each tuck and sewing across the fold. See page 21 for more information.

3. Press tucks up, toward the neckline. (Figure 7)

JOIN COLLAR FRONT AND BACK

1. With right sides together, pin each Collar Front (D) to two Collar Back (E) pieces at the shoulder seams, matching the tucks.

2. Stitch each shoulder seam. (Figure 8)

3. Press seams open.

4. Staystitch the neckline on each completed collar unit.

JOIN COLLAR AND COLLAR LINING

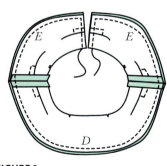

FIGURE 9

1. One of these collar units will form the outer collar, and one will form the collar lining. With right sides together, pin the outer collar to the collar lining, matching seams and edges.

2. Stitch the outer collar and collar lining together, beginning at the back neck edge, pivoting at the lower back edge, stitching around the entire outer edge, pivoting again, and sewing up the back edge to the neck. (Figure 9)

3. Notch the outer curves, trim and grade the seam allowance.

4. Turn the collar with rights sides out. Use the bamboo point turner to push out the points on the collar back (E). Press the seam flat.

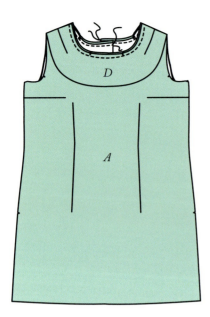

FIGURE 10

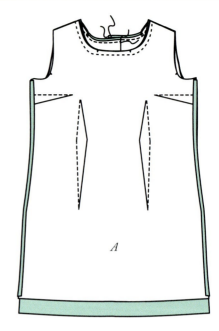

FIGURE 11

ATTACH COLLAR

1. With right side of the dress and the underside of the collar together, pin the collar to the neckline, matching the back edges of the collar with the circles.

2. Baste collar to the neckline. (Figure 10)

ATTACH LINING

1. With right sides together, pin lining to the dress shell at the neckline, matching seams, with the collar sandwiched between the shell and lining.

2. Stitch around the neckline, through all layers. (Figure 11)

3. Trim, grade and clip the inner curves of the seam allowance. Understitch the lining and press.

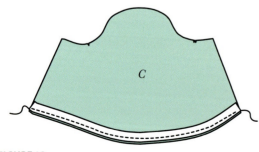

FIGURE 12

SEW BIAS TAPE TO SLEEVE HEM

1. Open out the bias tape completely and pin along each Sleeve (C) hem, with right sides together. Align the raw edge of the Sleeve (C) hem with the raw edge of the bias tape.

2. Stitch bias tape to the Sleeve (C) hem along the first fold of the bias tape (the fold line closest to the hem). (Figure 12)

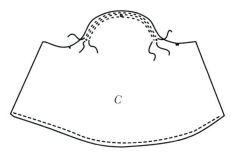

FIGURE 13

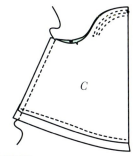

FIGURE 14

EASE SLEEVE CAP

1. Ease the sleeve cap between the two small circles. To do this, begin by using a long stitch length and stitch ⅝" (1.6 cm) from the edge between the small circles.

2. Stitch another row ½" (0.4cm) from the edge, and another ¾" (1cm) from the edge. Leave long thread tails which can be tugged to adjust ease. (Figure 13)

SEW SLEEVE UNDERARM

1. Fold out the bias tape and press it away from the sleeve.

2. Fold each sleeve piece right sides together. On each Sleeve (C), with right sides together and bias tape opened away from the Sleeve (C), stitch the underarm seam. Stitch all the way through the bias tape to join the ends. (Figure 14)

3. Finish the underarm seam and press open.

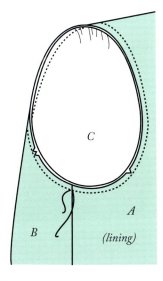

FIGURE 15

SET SLEEVE INTO ARMHOLE

1. Turn the lining to the inside so the wrong side of the lining and wrong side of the dress are together. Baste the lining to the dress at the armholes.

2. With right sides together, pin Sleeve (C) to armhole, including both the shell and lining layers. Match notches on Sleeve (C) to notches on armhole, match the large dot to the shoulder seam, and match the underarm seams while pinning.

3. Adjust the ease as necessary by tugging on the thread tails slightly and distributing the fullness evenly. Hand baste the Sleeve (C) into place.

4. Next, using a long stitch length, machine baste the Sleeve (C) to the armhole. (Figure 15)

5. Finally, stitch the Sleeve (C) into place. Finish the raw edge of this seam and press toward the Sleeve (C). Repeat this for the second Sleeve (C).

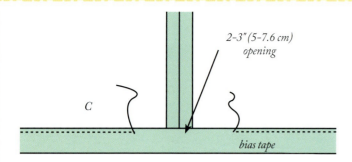

FIGURE 16

INSERT ELASTIC INTO SLEEVE HEM

1. On the lower edge of each sleeve, refold the bias tape and turn it to the inside to form a casing for the elastic.

2. Edgestitch the upper edge of the bias tape to the sleeve, leaving a 2" to 3" (5-7.6 cm) opening at the sleeve underarm, where you will insert the elastic. (Figure 16)

3. Cut a length of elastic that will fit comfortably yet snugly above your elbow. Cut a second piece the same length.

4. Attach a safety pin to the end of the elastic. Thread the elastic into the casing, safety pin first, and bring it back out the other side.

5. Stitch the ends of the elastic together.

6. Stitch the remaining opening in the bias tape casing closed.

7. Repeat for the second sleeve.

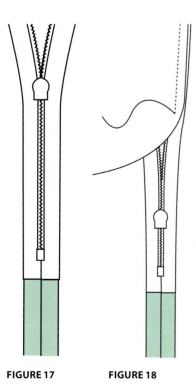

FIGURE 17   **FIGURE 18**

INSERT ZIPPER

1. Open the lining away from the shell of the dress.

2. Using an invisible zipper foot, sew in the invisible zipper between large circles, in the Dress Back (B) shell.

3. Stitch the center back seam closed below the zipper and press open. (Figure 17)

4. Turn the dress, and with the wrong side of the lining facing out, stitch the lining to the zipper tape, taking care not to sew through the dress. (Figure 18) Do this on both sides of the zipper. See pages 144-145 for details on sewing a lining to a zipper.

5. With right sides together, stitch the center back seam of the lining together beneath the zipper.

6. Hand sew the hook and eye at the back neck opening, above the zipper, on the inside of the dress.

HEM DRESS AND LINING

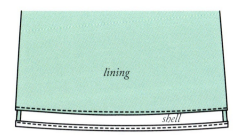

1. Try on the dress and adjust the hem to your preference. Adjust the length of the lining hem as well.

2. To hem the shell of the dress, turn hem under ¼" (6 mm) and press. Turn under again ⅜" (1 cm) and stitch to form a narrow hem.

3. Hem the lining in the same way. (Figure 19)

FIGURE 19

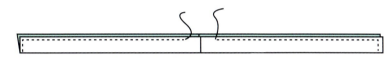

FIGURE 20

STITCH BELT

1. With right sides together, stitch Belt (F) pieces together along one short end. Press seam open.

2. Fold belt in half lengthwise, with right sides together.

3. Stitch along one short end, pivot at the corner, and stitch down the length, stopping 1" to 2" (2.5 to 5 cm) from the center back seam. Repeat on the other side. (Figure 20) This will leave you a gap in the center to turn the belt out.

4. Trim the seam and clip the corners to eliminate bulk.

5. Turn the belt right side out through the center opening.

6. On the opening, turn the seam allowance in and slipstitch it closed by hand. (See page 17.)

7. Press the belt flat.

GLOSSARY

Armscye: Armhole

Backstitch: Stitches sewn forward and back at the beginning and/or end of stitching in order to anchor the thread.

Baste: Long stitches done by hand or machine that temporarily hold fabric in place before sewing. They are removed once the final seam is in place.

Bias: Diagonal to the grain of the fabric. Fabric stretches along the bias.

Bias binding: A type of binding made from bias tape. The long edges are usually turned under and pressed.

Bias tape: Strips of fabric cut along the bias to make a stretchy tape that can be used for bindings and facings. The stretchiness helps the tape sew easily around curved areas.

Blind hem: A hem sewn with a blind stitch, which is barely visible from the outside of the garment.

Bodice: The top portion of a garment, above the waistline.

Clip: To help flatten a curved seam for sewing, clip inner curves by snipping into a curve at even intervals, being careful not to cut into the stitching.

Dart: A wedge shape that is stitched into fabric to create or control fullness in an area.

Ease: (1) Easing helps you sew a larger edge to a smaller edge, resulting in a slight fullness. To ease, use a long stitch length and stitch two rows parallel to each other. Leave long thread tails which can be tugged to adjust ease before you sew. (2) Ease is also the term for the extra room in a garment that allows for movement or looseness.

Edgestitch: Stitches sewn very close to the stitches on the seamline on the right side of fabric.

Facing: A piece that is sewn and then turned under to finish an edge.

Finish seam: Treating an edge, such as a seam, so that it's no longer prone to fraying. There are many ways to finish a seam or other raw edge, depending on the type of fabric you've chosen. For sturdier fabrics, trimming seams with pinking shears prevents fraying. For lighter fabrics, you use a zigzag along the edge. You could also try a turned-under seam, a bound edge or use a serger.

Gather: Like easing, gathering helps you sew a larger edge to a smaller edge, but results in much more fullness. See *Ease* for instructions.

Grade seam: Grading helps make seams that are pressed in a single direction less bulky. After you've sewn the seam, trim the seam allowance in half. Identify which seam allowance will be laying against the fabric, and trim this one in half again.

Grain: Usually refers to the lengthwise grain, or the threads of a fabric that run up and down, parallel to the selvage of fabric. The crosswise grain runs across, from selvage to selvage.

Hem: The lower edge of a garment. The hem is usually turned under and stitched.

Interfacing: A layer of material added to part of a garment to provide stiffness or stability. It's usually sandwiched between layers of fabric so that it's not visible.

Lining: Pieces sewn on the inside of a garment that mirror the outside. Lining fabrics are usually thin and smooth.

Nap: Fabrics with nap have fibers that stand away from the fabric, such as velvet. Because these fabrics usually appear different from different angles (i.e., they are "directional"), they must be cut using a one-way layout, with all pattern pieces facing the same direction.

Notch: There are two types of notches. The notches you see on the pattern help you to align pattern pieces when you're sewing. The other type of notches are ones you add yourself to help you sew curves. Notch outer curves on a seam by cutting wedge shapes into the seam allowance at even intervals, being careful not to cut into the stitching.

Pinking shears: A type of shear that cuts a zigzag line, which frays less than a straight cut. Pinking is a type of finishing.

Piping: Piping is used along seams as decoration, and consists of a cord wrapped in bias tape. Piping can be purchased, or made from your own fabric.

Pivot: Method for sewing when you reach a corner. Stop with the needle down at the corner, lift the presser foot, and rotate the fabric. Lower the presser foot and continue sewing in a new direction.

Pleat: A fold in the fabric that creates fullness.

Press: Placing an iron on fabric and applying pressure, without using the back-and-forth movement used in ironing.

Presser foot: The detachable portion of your sewing machine that the fabric moves under as it is sewn. Many types of presser feet exist for different uses and effects.

Right side/wrong side: The right side of a fabric is the side that will show on a finished garment. The wrong side will be on the inside.

Seam: The place where two pieces are joined together and stitched.

Seam allowance: The extra fabric that extends beyond the seam line. Most garments have a ⅝" (1.6 cm) seam allowance.

Selvage: The lengthwise edges of a fabric piece that do not fray.

Staystitch: A line of stitching on a piece that helps to stabilize the edge before it is sewn, preventing it from becoming distorted.

Tack: A few small stitches used to hold something in place. Often sewn by hand so they are invisible from the outside.

Topstitch: Similar to edgestitching, but more noticeable. Stitch on the outside, parallel to the seam, ¼" (6 mm) from the seam. Sew through fabric and seam allowance after pressing to help the seam lay flat.

Understitch: Understitching helps seams lie flat and prevents facings and linings from rolling to the outside of your garment. To understitch a facing, press the seam toward your facing. Stitch the seam to the facing very close to the seamline.

Warp: The lengthwise grain of a fabric (see *Grain*).

Weft: The crosswise grain of a fabric (see *Grain*).

INDEX

alterations
    common, 77
    fullness, 78, 79, 88–89
    how to make, 80
    to muslin, 74–76
    pivot, 78, 79, 82–87
    slash, 78, 79, 81

basting, 16
bias tape
    binding edges with, 136
    designing with, 137
    making, 138–139
blouse project, 147–153
body shape, 34, 35, 65, 66
bond paper, 72
bound edges, 136–137
bound seam, 142
bust
    alterations for, 88–89
    measurement, 70
buttonholes, 40

clipping, 22
corduroy, 121
cotton, 109, 113
croquis, 37
cutting
    fabrics, 43, 50–51
    layout, 44
    lines on patterns, 40, 41
    tools, 13, 51

darts, 40
    converted to seam, 67
    double-pointed, 21
    and fullness, 65, 66
    how to sew, 20
denim, 121
dress forms, 69
dresses, 91–101, 123–133, 159–169

ease, 64
embellishments, 101

fabric shears, 13, 51
fabrics, 103
    choosing, 104–107
    cutting, 50–51
    drape, 107
    fiber types, 108
    grain, 43, 110
    lining, 143
    with a nap, 44
    patterned, 46–47, 118–119
    pressing, 42
    prewashing, 42
    sheen, 106
    stretch, 105
    texture, 105
    trueing-up, 43
    types, 112–114
    warp, 110
    weft, 110
    weight, 106
facings, 22
faux fur, 120
fit, 61, 62, 63. *see also* darts
    ease, 64
    fullness, 65
    wrinkles, 74–75
fitting process, 68. see also sizing
flat felled seam, 141
French seam, 140
fullness
    alterations, 78, 79, 88, 89
    and darts, 65, 66
    and fit, 65
fundamentals, 9

gathers, 19, 67
grainlines, 40, 41

hip width, 83

inspiration, 30, 31
interfacing, 115

knits, 111

Licorice Dress, 159–169
linen, 109
linings
    adding, 144
    fabrics, 143
    and zippers, 144–145

marking tools, 13, 48, 49
measurements
    taking, 70
    tools for, 13
Meringue Skirt, 53–59
mood boards, 31
muslin
    adjusting, 74–76
    making, 73
    versus tissue paper, 68

needles, 12, 117
notching, 22, 99

Pastille Dress, 91–101
pattern paper, 44, 72
patterned fabrics, 118–119
patterns, 39
    instructions, 40, 41
    laying out pieces, 44, 45, 46–47
    symbols on, 40, 41
    tracing, 72
    transferring markings, 48–49
pinked seam, 142
pins, 12
plaids, 46–47, 118
plans, 29, 30, 31, 36. *see also* styles
pressing
    fabrics, 42
    pattern paper, 44, 72
    seams, 18
    tools, 14
princess seams, 67
prints, 118–119

quilting cottons, 113

rayon, 109
reference books, 77, 156–157
rotary cutters, 13, 51
ruffles, 19

seam allowances, 45, 59, 79
seam grading, 22, 59
seams
    finishing, 136–137, 140–142
    and fit, 67
    pressing open, 18
serged seam, 142
sewing hammer, 121
shoulder alterations, 77, 87
silks, 12, 108, 143
size chart, 171
sizing
    grading a curve, 71
    from measurements, 71
    on patterns, 41
sketchbooks, 31
sketches, 36, 37
skirt project, 53–59

skirts
    fullness alterations, 89
    length, 81
    pleats, 100
    sway back alteration, 82
    waist alterations, 85, 87
sleeves
    how to set, 26–27
    width alterations, 81
stabilizers, 50
stitches
    hand, 16–17
    machine, 15
stripes, 46–47, 118
styles, 33
    dressing for life, 34
    dressing for your shape, 34, 35
    personal approach to, 32
sway back, 82

Taffy Blouse, 147–153
thread, 12, 116
tissue fitting, 68
torso length, 70, 81
Truffle Dress, 123–133
tucks, 21

understitching, 22

velvet, 121

waist
    alterations for, 81, 84–87
    measurement, 70
    seam, 83
wearable muslin, 73
weaves, 111
wool, 108
wrinkles, 74–75

zippers
    centered, 24
    invisible, 23
    length, 25
    and linings, 144–145

SIZE CHART

	Bust Measurement	Waist Measurement	Hip Measurement
Size 0	33" (84cm)	25" (63cm)	35" (89cm)
Size 2	33" (84cm)	26" (66cm)	36" (91cm)
Size 4	35" (89cm)	27" (69cm)	37" (94cm)
Size 6	36" (91cm)	28" (71cm)	38" (97cm)
Size 8	37" (94cm)	29" (74cm)	39" (99cm)
Size 10	38½" (98cm)	30½" (78cm)	40½" (103cm)
Size 12	40" (102cm)	32" (81cm)	42" (107cm)
Size 14	42" (107cm)	34" (86cm)	44" (112cm)
Size 16	44" (112cm)	36" (91cm)	46" (117cm)
Size 18	46" (117cm)	38" (97cm)	48" (122cm)

DEDICATION

To my grandmothers: Ida (Nonna), who taught me to use my first sewing machine, and Ruth (Nana), who loved clothes even more than I do. I aspire to be as kind, creative, warm and generous as both of you.

ACKNOWLEDGMENTS

Thank you to all the many people who made this book possible. Caitlin Clark, for being an excellent first mate, a tireless stitcher, and letting me talk about my cats so much. Thanks to Rachel Rector for all her creativity, not to mention just being a ray of sunshine in the studio. You both make hard work a total joy.

Thank you to my editor, Vanessa Lyman, for all of your support and encouragement throughout. You totally got it, and I couldn't have hoped for a better match.

To the lovely ladies who prettied up this book with their incredible talent: Lisa Warninger for her stunning photography, Chelsea Fuss for her gorgeous photo styling and prop magic, and Kassandra Sommerville of The Ginger Suite Salon for the beautiful hair and makeup. Thanks also to Jen Alfieri Adams and the wonderful people at The Ace Hotel for the wonderful photo location.

Thank you to all the women who tested out patterns and gave me feedback. Meredith Neal, my first round tester: You rule. Thanks also to Mena, Hillary, Katie, Sunni, Jen, Heather, Melissa, Jaime and Casey. Your thoughts were invaluable.

Jade, Ari, Catherine and Amber for brightening this book with your beautiful smiles.

Last, thanks to my family. To Kenn, the most supportive husband and best friend I could have hoped for. Mom and Dad, for always making me feel loved and capable of anything. To Nonna, for teaching me to make my first dress. And to Rachel, David and the rest of my wonderful family for always keeping me laughing.

METRIC CONVERSION CHART

To convert	to	multiply by
Inches	Centimeters	2.54
Centimeters	Inches	0.4
Feet	Centimeters	30.5
Centimeters	Feet	0.03
Yards	Meters	0.9
Meters	Yards	1.1

The instructions and patterns in this book were designed with Imperial measurements. Though metric conversions are supplied, for best results, use Imperial measurements.

The Colette Sewing Handbook Copyright © 2011 by Sarai Mitnick. Manufactured in China. All rights reserved. The patterns and drawings in this book are for the personal use of the reader. By permission of the author and publisher, they may be either hand-traced or photocopied to make single copies, but under no circumstances may they be resold or republished. No part of this book may be reproduced in any form or by any electronic or mechanical means including information storage and retrieval systems without permission in writing from the publisher, except by a reviewer who may quote brief passages in a review. Published by Krause Publications, a division of F+W Media, Inc., 4700 East Galbraith Road, Cincinnati, Ohio, 45236. (800) 289-0963. First Edition.

www.fwmedia.com

15 14 13 12   5 4 3

DISTRIBUTED IN CANADA BY FRASER DIRECT
100 Armstrong Avenue
Georgetown, ON, Canada L7G 5S4
Tel: (905) 877-4411

DISTRIBUTED IN THE U.K. AND EUROPE BY F&W MEDIA INTERNATIONAL
Brunel House, Newton Abbot, Devon, TQ12 4PU, England
Tel: (+44) 1626 323200, Fax: (+44) 1626 323319
Email: enquiries@fwmedia.com

DISTRIBUTED IN AUSTRALIA BY CAPRICORN LINK
P.O. Box 704, S. Windsor NSW, 2756 Australia
Tel: (02) 4577-3555

SRN: Y1290
ISBN-13: 978-1-4402-1545-2

ABOUT THE AUTHOR

Sarai Mitnick is the founder and designer behind Colette Patterns, a line of classic sewing patterns known for sweet details and excellent instruction. With a background in User Experience, Sarai wanted to create patterns that were a joy to use and learn from. Along with a small team of talented stitchers and bloggers, she now runs Colette Patterns from a lovely sunlit studio in Portland, Oregon. When she's not sewing (or writing about sewing), Sarai enjoys petting her cats (Basil and Colette), growing vegetables, drinking cocktails, traveling, knitting, making good food, reading and exploring the beautiful city she calls home. Visit her at www.colettepatterns.com, or at her personal blog, www.sweetsassafras.org.

Edited by Vanessa Lyman
Designed by Michelle Thompson
of Fold & Gather Design
Production coordinated by Greg Nock
Photography by Lisa Warninger
Photostyling by Chelsea Fuss
Step-by-step photography by Christine Polomsky

NEEDLE? THREAD? FABRIC?

STORE.MARTHAPULLEN.COM IS WHERE YOU GO TO SEW! FIND INSPIRATION AND INSTRUCTION FOR ALL STITCHERS, WHETHER YOU SEW BY MACHINE OR HAND!

A COMMUNITY OF CRAFTERS

 Visit us on Facebook:
www.facebook.com/fwcraft

 Join us on Twitter: @fwcraft

 Share with us on Flickr:
www.flickr.com/northlightcrafts

WHETHER YOU'RE MASTERING TECHNIQUE OR LOOKING FOR FUN PROJECTS, KRAUSE PUBLICATIONS CAN HELP YOU ON YOUR WAY TO BECOMING A MODERN SEAMSTRESS!

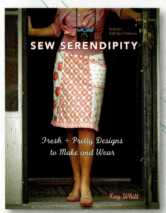

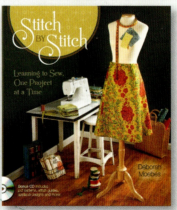